CONTENTS

▶ **The Best Movies: A to Z**   **5**

▶ **Movies by Topic**   **105**

▶ **Movies by Age**   **125**

▶ **Common Sense Seal Honorees**   **143**

www.commonsense.org

THE BEST MOVIES: A TO Z

101 Dalmatians

Lovable cartoon classic with cute dogs and a mean villain.

 age 5+ ★★★★★

Cruella De Vil, one of the most memorable female villains in movie history, kidnaps 101 Dalmatians so she can make a fur coat. But Dalmatian adults Pongo and Perdita, with the help of their animal friends, undertake a daring rescue. The puppies are adorable, and the movie is exciting, funny, and fun.

 Positive messages

 Positive role models

 Violence & scariness

Director: Clyde Geronimi
Cast: Betty Lou Gerson, Cate Bauer, Rod Taylor
Running time: 79 minutes
Release year: 1961
Genre: Animation
MPAA rating: G

FAMILIES CAN TALK ABOUT ...
What makes Cruella scary? What similarities do many movie villains share?

About a Boy

Grant grows a heart in Hornby-book pic; teens+.

 age 14+ ★★★★☆

Will wants to live a life of no attachments, but a troubled 12-year-old boy ultimately insists on becoming the closest thing to a friend Will has ever known. A purely satisfying and enjoyable film, with a superb performance of great honesty, subtlety, and comic timing from Hugh Grant.

 Positive messages

 Sexy stuff

 Language

Director: Chris Weitz, Paul Weitz
Cast: Hugh Grant, Nicholas Hoult, Toni Collette
Running time: 102 minutes
Release year: 2002
Genre: Drama
MPAA rating: PG-13

FAMILIES CAN TALK ABOUT ...
What roles do friendships and other relationships play in our lives? Why is it important to Will not to have any relationships? What does he learn in the end?

The Adventures of Milo and Otis

Lovable pet tale about friendship despite differences.

 age 5+

Newborn Milo, a real scamp of a kitten, meets timid puppy Otis, and it's the start of a hilarious friendship. Told with voice-overs by Dudley Moore, the story shows the pair leaving home for the first time, undergoing tests of their courage and friendship and returning home to accept responsibility.

 Positive messages

 Positive role models

Director: Masanori Hata
Cast: Dudley Moore
Running time: 76 minutes
Release year: 1989
Genre: Drama
MPAA rating: G

FAMILIES CAN TALK ABOUT ...

How do Milo and Otis prove their loyalty to one another? What lessons can we learn from them?

The Adventures of Robin Hood

Errol Flynn stars in swashbuckling family delight.

 age 8+

Errol Flynn stars as Lord Robin of Locksley, who's enraged at the mistreatment of his people. What's fascinating about this version is the distinctly 1930s American sensibility — it's less a sweet and cartoonish fairy tale than it is a thinly veiled attack on capitalism and an absentee leader.

 Positive messages

 Violence & scariness

Director: Michael Curtiz, William Keighley
Cast: Basil Rathbone, Claude Rains, Errol Flynn, Olivia de Havilland
Running time: 102 minutes
Release year: 1938
Genre: Action/Adventure
MPAA rating: PG

FAMILIES CAN TALK ABOUT ...

What does Robin Hood represent? Why is the idea of resistance to corrupt authority important?

Akeelah and the Bee

Inspiring drama about a champion speller; OK for tweens.

 age 8+ ★★★★☆

Resolute, self-protecting 11-year-old Akeelah has a gift for spelling. This film traces her delicate, courageous growing up and her evolving relationships with an adult friend and her mom, but it's her relationships with other kids that stand out. Intelligent and charming.

 Positive messages

 Positive role models

Director: Doug Atchison
Cast: Angela Bassett, Keke Palmer, Laurence Fishburne
Running time: 112 minutes
Release year: 2006
Genre: Drama
MPAA rating: PG

FAMILIES CAN TALK ABOUT ...
How does Akeelah's success inspire others to feel part of a group, as her spelling becomes a community project?

Aladdin

A magic carpet ride of a movie from Disney.

 age 6+ ★★★★★

Street urchin Aladdin woos Princess Jasmine by pretending to be a prince, with the help of an exuberant blue genie. But before the story ends happily ever after, Aladdin must tell Jasmine the truth — and defeat evil royal advisor Jafar! A very entertaining Disney movie.

 Positive messages

 Violence & scariness

Director: John Musker, Ron Clements
Cast: Linda Larkin, Robin Williams, Scott Weinger
Running time: 90 minutes
Release year: 1992
Genre: Animation
MPAA rating: G

FAMILIES CAN TALK ABOUT ...
Can people be both good and bad? How do we learn from our mistakes?

Alice in Wonderland

Surreal animated Disney classic with mild peril.

 age 4+ ★★★★☆

Alice follows a white rabbit, fully dressed and muttering about being late, down a hole to Wonderland, whose inhabitants are often rude, unfriendly, and even hostile. Disney's classic animated interpretation of Lewis Carroll's tale is a great "starter" before more mature versions.

 Positive messages

Director: Clyde Geronimi
Cast: Ed Wynn, Kathryn Beaumont, Sterling Holloway
Running time: 75 minutes
Release year: 1951
Genre: Animation
MPAA rating: G

FAMILIES CAN TALK ABOUT ...

Which of the movie's wild characters is your favorite? Do you think they're meant to represent anything in particular?

Almost Famous

Great, but lots of sex, drugs, and rock 'n' roll.

 age 16+ ★★★★★

In Cameron Crowe's love letter to rock music, teenager William gets a big break when Lester Bang, editor of *Creem*, hires him to cover a Black Sabbath concert. That leads to an assignment at *Rolling Stone* that changes his life. A clear, affectionate eye for 1970s styles and attitudes.

 Positive messages

 Sexy stuff

 Language

 Drinking, drugs, & smoking

Director: Cameron Crowe
Cast: Jason Lee, Kate Hudson, Patrick Fugit
Running time: 122 minutes
Release year: 2000
Genre: Drama
MPAA rating: R

FAMILIES CAN TALK ABOUT ...

How do you think real musicians and other celebrities handle sudden fame and fortune? How has media attention to stars changed since the movie's time period?

Amadeus

Lavish, award-winning film with mature themes.

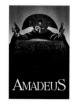

 age 13+ ★★★★☆

This multiple Oscar winner uses the real-life figures and the music of Wolfgang Amadeus Mozart and lesser-known composer Antonio Salieri in an ornate, if lengthy, tale of envy, talent, and wicked manipulation. Some scholars may wince at the distorted history — but the movie rocks.

 Positive messages

 Violence & scariness

 Sexy stuff

 Language

 Drinking, drugs, & smoking

Director: Milos Forman
Cast: Elizabeth Berridge, F. Murray Abraham, Tom Hulce
Running time: 158 minutes
Release year: 1984
Genre: Drama
MPAA rating: R

FAMILIES CAN TALK ABOUT ...

What sources do you use to learn about history? When do you question the accuracy of a historical tale?

American Graffiti

Coming-of-age classic still a must-see for teens.

 age 13+ ★★★★★

The music! The clothes! The cars! Unknown director George Lucas set a standard for teen movies in 1962. Most of the young actors are famous now — Ron Howard, Harrison Ford, Richard Dreyfus, Suzanne Sommers, Mackenzie Phillips — and the soundtrack is a virtual greatest-hits collection from the era.

 Language

 Drinking, drugs, & smoking

Director: George Lucas
Cast: Cindy Williams, Harrison Ford, Richard Dreyfuss
Running time: 110 minutes
Release year: 1973
Genre: Comedy
MPAA rating: PG

FAMILIES CAN TALK ABOUT ...

How does this film compare with contempory movies about high school kids? How is it different? The same?

Anne of Green Gables

Faithful, sensitive take on classic novel is great for kids.

  age 7+ ★★★★★

Anne Shirley, a 13-year-old orphan, is sent to live with a new family in picturesque Avonlea. They expected a boy, but Anne, hilariously outspoken and strong-willed, transcends her issues and fulfills her dreams. Gorgeous to look at and brimming with simple truths about love, friendship, and family.

 Positive messages

 Positive role models

Director: Kevin Sullivan
Cast: Colleen Dewhurst, Megan Follows, Richard Farnsworth
Running time: 199 minutes
Release year: 1986
Genre: Drama
MPAA rating: NR

FAMILIES CAN TALK ABOUT ...

Is Anne like any kids you know in real life? How do you think she'd be different if the movie was set in modern times?

Annie (1982)

Tale of cute orphan is great for the whole family.

 age 6+ ★★★★★

Spunky, red-haired orphan Annie dreams of the day her parents will retrieve her. With outstanding performances by Albert Finney, Carol Burnett, Bernadette Peters, and Tim Curry, this classic musical will have you singing show tunes — and maybe dreaming of a dog as loyal as Sandy.

 Positive messages

 Positive role models

 Violence & scariness

 Drinking, drugs, & smoking

Director: John Huston
Cast: Aileen Quinn, Albert Finney, Carol Burnett
Running time: 127 minutes
Release year: 1982
Genre: Musical
MPAA rating: PG

FAMILIES CAN TALK ABOUT ...

What makes Annie a role model? What about the other characters? Why is her story so enduringly popular?

Annie Hall

Classic comedy about relationships has mature themes.

annie hall

 age 14+ ★★★★☆

Woody Allen's sophisticated take on relationships is lively and fleet, with a plethora of one-liners and hilarious, attention-getting narrative devices, such as flashbacks that let the adult Woody go back to his elementary school. Watchable for older teens but not for kids (casual sex and drug use).

 Sexy stuff

 Language

 Drinking, drugs, & smoking

Director: Woody Allen
Cast: Carol Kane, Diane Keaton, Woody Allen
Running time: 99 minutes
Release year: 1977
Genre: Comedy
MPAA rating: PG

FAMILIES CAN TALK ABOUT ...

What are the hallmarks of Woody Allen's style of filmmaking? How does this one compare to his other movies?

Apollo 13

Thrilling, heartwarming, scary, and superb.

APOLLO 13

 age 12+ ★★★★★

Tom Hanks plays astronaut-hero Jim Lovell in this true story of the mission to the moon that almost left three astronauts stranded in space when an oxygen tank exploded. With masterful performances and impeccable technical authenticity, it's a thrilling, heartening tale of the triumph of smart guys.

 Positive messages

 Positive role models

 Language

Director: Ron Howard
Cast: Bill Paxton, Gary Sinise, Tom Hanks
Running time: 140 minutes
Release year: 1995
Genre: Drama
MPAA rating: PG

FAMILIES CAN TALK ABOUT ...

Even if you already know how it ends, this movie is extremely suspenseful. How do the filmmakers achieve that?

The Avengers

Heroes work together in explosive comic-book adventure.

 age 13+ ★★★★☆

When a powerful villain appears on Earth to find an artifact that holds limitless energy, the head of secret organization SHIELD calls in the toughest team he can find: the Avengers. Quick-witted and nuanced, the film takes the best of the superhero genre and dishes it out in a fanboy-pleasing way.

💬 Positive messages

👤 Positive role models

💥 Violence & scariness

💲 Consumerism

Director: Joss Whedon
Cast: Chris Evans, Chris Hemsworth, Robert Downey Jr.
Running time: 143 minutes
Release year: 2012
Genre: Action/Adventure
MPAA rating: PG-13

FAMILIES CAN TALK ABOUT ...

How does the fact that much of the violence in this movie is larger than life affect its impact? How is it different watching invading aliens get hurt than human characters?

Babe

Heartwarming farm story is touching and a bit scary.

 age 6+ ★★★★★

Babe is an endearing little pig raised by sheepdogs who befriends the animals on a farm and ultimately becomes a herder himself, triumphing against some pretty steep odds. It's a tale about making a place for yourself in the world, and it was one of the best-loved family movie of the 1990s.

💬 Positive messages

👤 Positive role models

💥 Violence & scariness

Director: Chris Noonan
Cast: Christine Cavanaugh, Hugo Weaving, James Cromwell
Running time: 91 minutes
Release year: 1995
Genre: Comedy
MPAA rating: G

FAMILIES CAN TALK ABOUT ...

How would this movie be different if it were animated? Why do you think animation changes the way we experience a movie?

Back to the Future

'80s time-travel favorite has laughs, romance, action.

 age 10+ ★★★★★

This 1980s blockbuster mixes science fiction with romantic comedy as Marty McFly travels back to the 1950s via a time machine, accidentally interfering with his parents' courtship. Now he must aid his father in attracting his mother to ensure his existence. Exuberant and lighthearted.

 Positive messages

 Positive role models

 Violence & scariness

 Sexy stuff

 Language

Director: Robert Zemeckis
Cast: Christopher Lloyd, Lea Thompson, Michael J. Fox
Running time: 116 minutes
Release year: 1985
Genre: Science Fiction
MPAA rating: PG

FAMILIES CAN TALK ABOUT ...

What do Marty and George learn during the movie? How can people defend themselves without resorting to violence?

Bambi

Disney's original circle-of-life story.

 age 5+ ★★★★★

Told mostly with music and animation, the story centers on wide-eyed deer Bambi, who must find a way to endure after hunters kill his mother. Supported by his friends, Bambi grows into a strong buck and a leader of the forest. Symphonic and choral pieces add grace and elegance to a timeless film.

 Positive messages

Positive role models

Violence & scariness

Director: David Hand
Cast: Hardie Albright, Peter Behn, Stan Alexander
Running time: 70 minutes
Release year: 1942
Genre: Animation
MPAA rating: G

FAMILIES CAN TALK ABOUT ...

Some pretty sad stuff happens in this movie. Why do you think the writers chose to include those parts? How did they affect you?

Barbershop

Charming ensemble comedy for teens.

 age 13+ ★★★★☆

Calvin (Ice Cube) spends the day trying to buy back his family's barbershop once he learns the loan shark he sold it to plans to turn it into a "gentlemen's club." This unassuming ensemble comedy has a surprisingly gentle and heartfelt center, and it's impossible not to be charmed by it.

 Positive messages

 Positive role models

#! Language

Director: Tim Story
Cast: Cedric the Entertainer, Ice Cube, Sean Patrick Thomas
Running time: 102 minutes
Release year: 2002
Genre: Comedy
MPAA rating: PG-13

FAMILIES CAN TALK ABOUT ...

What is an ensemble comedy? Can you think of some other examples?

Beauty and the Beast

The ultimate makeover story has strong, positive messages.

 age 5+ ★★★★★

When a prince turns away an ugly, old woman selling apples, she casts a spell that turns him into a beast. He must find someone to love him to undo the enchantment ... and along comes Belle. Disney's crowning achievement won an Oscar nomination and a Golden Globe for Best Picture.

 Positive messages

 Positive role models

 Violence & scariness

Director: Gary Trousdale, Kirk Wise
Cast: Paige O'Hara, Richard White, Robby Benson
Running time: 90 minutes
Release year: 1991
Genre: Animation
MPAA rating: G

FAMILIES CAN TALK ABOUT ...

What were Belle and Beast's first impressions of each other? What did they discover about each other as their relationship grew?

Bend It Like Beckham

Superb tale of a girl's struggle for her dreams.

 age 13+ ★★★★☆

A color-drenched fairy tale for any girl whose athletic endeavors were ever questioned by conservative parents. Spunky and easy to watch, it centers on second-generation Indian families in England striving to maintain traditions, but the universal theme is following your bliss no matter the hurdle.

 Positive messages

 Positive role models

 Language

Director: Gurinder Chadha
Cast: Jonathan Rhys Meyers, Keira Knightley, Pariminder Nagra
Running time: 112 minutes
Release year: 2003
Genre: Comedy
MPAA rating: PG-13

FAMILIES CAN TALK ABOUT ...

Why do you think Jess feels she can't talk to her family about her love of sports? What do she and her family learn in the end?

Big

Wonderful story with some very mature material.

 age 13+ ★★★★☆

Fed up with being little, 12-year-old Josh makes a wish at a fair's mechanical swami booth and wakes the next morning in a man's body (Tom Hanks). Strong, earnest performances make the incredible credible. Intelligent and inventive. (Rated PG before PG-13 existed, the film has mature material.)

 Positive messages

 Sexy stuff

 Language

 Drinking, drugs, & smoking

Director: Penny Marshall
Cast: Elizabeth Perkins, Robert Loggia, Tom Hanks
Running time: 104 minutes
Release year: 1988
Genre: Comedy
MPAA rating: PG

FAMILIES CAN TALK ABOUT ...

What are the best things about being a kid? What are the advantages of being an adult?

Big Hero 6

Awesome origin story is action-packed, deals with grief.

 age 7+

A captivating superhero adventure for the entire family that focuses on the power of brotherhood, friendship, and using your gifts to help others, with a theme of coping with grief. Refreshingly diverse cast; inflatable robot Baymax is impossible not to love.

 Positive messages

 Positive role models

 Violence & scariness

Director: Chris Williams, Don Hall

Cast: Damon Wayans Jr., Genesis Rodriguez, Jamie Chung

Running time: 102 minutes

Release year: 2014

Genre: Animation

MPAA rating: PG

FAMILIES CAN TALK ABOUT ...

Why do you think so many young movie characters are orphans? What makes Hiro different from the typical pop-culture orphan?

Billy Elliot

Terrific story of young ballet dancer has strong language.

age 13+

In 1984 England, the police come to the small mining town of Durham to keep order during a strike. Amid the tension, 11-year-old Billy, whose main sport is boxing, is pulled into a ballet lesson. His father is furious and tells him to quit — but Billy has to dance. Tender, funny, and touching.

 Positive messages

Positive role models

Sexy stuff

Language

Drinking, drugs, & smoking

Director: Stephen Daldry

Cast: Gary Lewis, Jamie Bell, Julie Walters

Running time: 111 minutes

Release year: 2000

Genre: Drama

MPAA rating: R

FAMILIES CAN TALK ABOUT ...

Why was Billy's interest in ballet so terrifying to him? What made him change his mind?

The Black Stallion

Breathtakingly beautiful and magical horse movie.

 age 8+ ★★★★★

Pauline Kael said this "may be the greatest children's movie ever made." After a shipwreck, only Alec and a horse survive. Back at home, the horse runs to a farm, where Alec meets a trainer (Mickey Rooney). They enter the formerly wild horse in a race. Breathtakingly beautiful, genuinely magic.

 Positive messages

 Positive role models

 Violence & scariness

Director: Carroll Ballard
Cast: Kelly Reno, Mickey Rooney, Teri Garr
Running time: 118 minutes
Release year: 1979
Genre: Drama
MPAA rating: G

FAMILIES CAN TALK ABOUT ...

Why does the horse trust Alec? Why is it important for Alec to win the race? What lessons does Alec learn from his experiences?

Blade Runner

A dark, philosophical sci-fi drama for older teens.

 age 16+ ★★★★☆

In futuristic, dystopian L.A., Rick Deckard, a former Blade Runner, is called out of retirement to kill a gang of rogue replicants, robots that look just like humans — but by now they've developed human emotions and a lust for life. Considered one of the greatest science-fiction films of all time.

 Violence & scariness

 Sexy stuff

 Drinking, drugs, & smoking

Director: Ridley Scott
Cast: Daryl Hannah, Harrison Ford, Sean Young
Running time: 117 minutes
Release year: 1982
Genre: Science Fiction
MPAA rating: R

FAMILIES CAN TALK ABOUT ...

How does Blade Runner's bleak urban vision of the future differ from that in other dystopian books and movies?

Boyhood

Unique, affecting, mature drama about life and growing up.

 age 15+ ★★★★★

This extraordinary drama was filmed over the course of 12 years, following the main character from age 5 to 18. It has its share of mature content and themes (strong language, abuse, alcoholism, drugs), but ultimately it's a very special movie that, if teens and parents watch together, could spark fascinating discussions about life.

 Language

 Drinking, drugs, & smoking

Director: Richard Linklater
Cast: Ellar Coltrane, Ethan Hawke, Patricia Arquette
Running time: 166 minutes
Release year: 2014
Genre: Drama
MPAA rating: R

FAMILIES CAN TALK ABOUT ...

Did you have any difficulty watching a movie of this length and with this format? How is it different from more mainstream movies?

The Breakfast Club

Socially relevant '80s teen flick.

 age 15+ ★★★★☆

Five high school students, who rank high and low in popularity, are forced to spend nine hours together in Saturday detention. They eventually come to realize that, underneath the trappings of the social scene, the problems they face are more similar than they think. A John Hughes classic.

 Sexy stuff

 Language

 Drinking, drugs, & smoking

Director: John Hughes
Cast: Ally Sheedy, Anthony Michael Hall, Emilio Estevez, Judd Nelson, Molly Ringwald
Running time: 97 minutes
Release year: 1985
Genre: Drama
MPAA rating: R

FAMILIES CAN TALK ABOUT ...

Why is this movie considered a teen classic? If you could update it, how would you do it, and whom would you cast?

Bringing Up Baby

Classic screwball comedy with loads of tame laughs.

 age 8+ ★★★★★

Cary Grant, Katherine Hepburn, and a leopard star in what's generally considered the ultimate example of the screwball comedy. Masterful director Howard Hawks pulls off an outlandish plot at breakneck speed with fabulous witty repartee and romantic tension between the perfectly cast leads.

 Positive messages

 Positive role models

Director: Howard Hawks

Cast: Cary Grant, Charles Ruggles, Katharine Hepburn

Running time: 102 minutes

Release year: 1938

Genre: Comedy

MPAA rating: NR

FAMILIES CAN TALK ABOUT ...

What are the elements of a "screwball comedy"? What are other comedic styles? Which do you prefer?

Casablanca

Brief violence and lots of tension in top-notch classic.

 age 10+ ★★★★★

This iconic love story follows a hardboiled American nightclub owner (Humphrey Bogart) and his ex-lover (Ingrid Bergman) in French-controlled Casablanca in early WWII. A story of love, betrayal, sacrifice, and narrow escapes, with the most memorable airport tarmac scene in film history.

 Positive messages

 Positive role models

 Violence & scariness

Director: Michael Curtiz

Cast: Humphrey Bogart, Ingrid Bergman, Paul Henreid

Running time: 102 minutes

Release year: 1942

Genre: Romance

MPAA rating: NR

FAMILIES CAN TALK ABOUT ...

What makes a movie stand the test of time? Which contemporary movies do you think will last?

A Charlie Brown Christmas

The Peanuts gang in a classic Christmas special.

 age 3+   ★★★★★

Charlie Brown discovers the true meaning of Christmas when he buys and transforms a forlorn little tree. Simple drawings, a gently meandering story, Charles Schultz's beloved characters, and a lively musical score make this a movie the entire family will want to watch every year.

 Positive messages

 Positive role models

Director: Bill Melendez
Cast: Bill Melendez, Peter Robbins, Sally Dryer
Running time: 30 minutes
Release year: 1965
Genre: Animation
MPAA rating: NR

FAMILIES CAN TALK ABOUT ...

Does the true meaning of Christmas get lost in materialism? How could you work against that — either in your family or in society?

Charlotte's Web (2006)

Enchanting take on a beloved children's classic.

 age 5+   ★★★★★

The other animals are reluctant to befriend Wilbur, a pig fated to be served up as the humans' Christmas dinner. But Wilbur is so sweet, curious, and affable that they're won over — and Charlotte, the barn spider, decides to find a way to save his life. Thoughtful, entertaining, and enchanting.

 Positive messages

 Positive role models

Director: Gary Winick
Cast: Dakota Fanning, Dominic Scott Kay, Julia Roberts
Running time: 97 minutes
Release year: 2006
Genre: Drama
MPAA rating: G

FAMILIES CAN TALK ABOUT ...

How do the animals come to see one another as friends, even though at first they're put off by their differences?

Chicken Run

Charming animated escape tale has some peril, scares.

 age 7+   ★★★★☆

A brave chicken plots an escape from a Yorkshire chicken farm. The world is enchantingly believable, and the chickens and side characters are highly individual and wildly funny. Parents and kids alike will delight in the Rube Goldberg-like machines and split-second action sequences.

 Positive messages

 Positive role models

 Violence & scariness

Director: Nick Park

Cast: Julia Sawalha, Mel Gibson, Miranda Richardson

Running time: 84 minutes

Release year: 2000

Genre: Animation

MPAA rating: G

FAMILIES CAN TALK ABOUT ...

How does the movie's cartoonish violence heighten both the comedic and scary parts?

Children of Heaven

Excellent subtitled Iranian coming-of-age story.

 age 10+   ★★★★★

This Oscar-nominated film is a fascinating story of contemporary Iran and a universal coming-of-age tale about the bonds of family as well as the specific circumstances of a poor family trying to make ends meet. A beautifully rendered encapsulation of the trials and suspense of childhood.

 Positive messages

 Positive role models

Director: Majid Majidi

Cast: Amir Farrokh Hashemian, Bahare Sadiqi, Mohammad Amir Naji

Running time: 89 minutes

Release year: 1999

Genre: Drama

MPAA rating: PG

FAMILIES CAN TALK ABOUT ...

How is the relationship between Ali and his sister Zahra similar to that of brothers and sisters everywhere?

Chitty Chitty Bang Bang

A fantastical car story custom-made for kids.

 age 6+ ★★★★

In this musical based on an Ian Fleming novel, co-written by Roald Dahl, and scored by the Mary Poppins writers, Dick Van Dyke is a down-on-his-luck inventor who buys a used car for his kids — but the dream machine flies, floats, and perhaps even thinks for itself. The stuff of fantasies.

 Positive messages

 Positive role models

 Violence & scariness

Director: Ken Hughes

Cast: Dick Van Dyke, Lionel Jeffries, Sally Ann Howes

Running time: 144 minutes

Release year: 1968

Genre: Musical

MPAA rating: G

FAMILIES CAN TALK ABOUT ...

What would you do with a car like Chitty Chitty Bang Bang? What kinds of things would you like to invent?

A Christmas Story

Wonderful antidote to cutesy holiday tales; some swearing.

 age 8+ ★★★★★

In 1940s Indiana, 9-year-old Ralphie is consumed by one wish: to get a Red Ryder BB gun for Christmas. Part of the film's appeal is the authentic period detail, but what most engages is the timeless details of childhood, including bullies and double-dog dares. A funny antidote to cutesy TV specials.

 Positive messages

 Language

Director: Bob Clark

Cast: Darren McGavin, Melinda Dillon, Peter Billingsley

Running time: 98 minutes

Release year: 1983

Genre: Comedy

MPAA rating: PG

FAMILIES CAN TALK ABOUT ...

What makes people act like bullies? How do you think life might change for the bully in this movie after Ralphie fights him?

Cinderella

Sweet fairy-tale classic for little princes and princesses.

 age 5+ ★★★★★

Charles Perrault's fairy tale comes to life with gorgeously detailed and inventive animation. Little ones might cringe at the wicked stepsisters and stepmom, and Cinderella is a passive heroine rescued by a prince, but Disney's vivid and endearing characters win the day with memorable songs.

 Positive role models

Director: Clyde Geronimi, Hamilton Luske, Wilfred Jackson
Cast: Eleanor Audley, Ilene Woods, Verna Felton
Running time: 74 minutes
Release year: 1950
Genre: Animation
MPAA rating: G

FAMILIES CAN TALK ABOUT ...

Why do you think the stepsisters are ugly and Cinderella is pretty? What would the story be like if Cinderella was ugly?

Cinema Paradiso

Charming Italian film about friendship, movies.

 age 13+ ★★★★☆

Altar boy Salvatore finds a substitute for the father he lost to war at the movie theater: Alfredo reluctantly teaches him how to operate the projector — but then he develops higher hopes for his surrogate son, who finally leaves to become a filmmaker. The perfect introduction to foreign films.

 Positive messages

 Sexy stuff

Director: Giuseppe Tornatore
Cast: Antonella Attili, Enzo Cannavale, Isa Danieli
Running time: 121 minutes
Release year: 1989
Genre: Drama
MPAA rating: PG

FAMILIES CAN TALK ABOUT ...

How does Alfredo help Salvatore gain the confidence to pursue his passion? Who are your own mentors?

Citizen Kane

Classic should be required for any movie lover.

 age 12+ ★★★★★

This serious film won't appeal to young kids, but for teens it's the must-see portrait of an early 20th-century media tycoon. Made in 1941, it's thought to be the best movie of all time, both for its audacious techniques and for the depth of its characterization. Orson Welles stars and directs.

 Positive messages

 Drinking, drugs, & smoking

Director: Orson Welles

Cast: Agnes Moorehead, Joseph Cotten, Orson Welles

Running time: 119 minutes

Release year: 1941

Genre: Drama

MPAA rating: NR

FAMILIES CAN TALK ABOUT ...

Kane used his newspaper to influence politics and stir up the public's interest in war. Do newspapers and other news media still do that?

Close Encounters of the Third Kind

Suspenseful, thoughtful alien-encounter classic.

 age 8+ ★★★★★

Inexplicably drawn to Devil's Tower, Roy and Jillian realize they're not the only ones who feel they've been called there. An enormous spacecraft shows up and returns humans taken over decades, and Roy boldly boards the ship in an intergalactic exchange program. A thrilling adventure story.

 Positive messages

 Positive role models

 Violence & scariness

 Language

Director: Steven Spielberg

Cast: Francois Truffaut, Melinda Dillon, Richard Dreyfuss

Running time: 132 minutes

Release year: 1977

Genre: Science Fiction

MPAA rating: PG

FAMILIES CAN TALK ABOUT ...

How are aliens usually portrayed in the movies? What does this film do differently?

Clueless

Charming, funny take on Jane Austen's *Emma*.

 age 14+ ★★★★☆

After one successful attempt at matchmaking, Cher decides to make over the new girl at school, with disastrous results. Meanwhile, her own love life is confused, but when she starts being honest with herself she sees what she really wants. Loosely based on Jane Austen's *Emma*.

 Positive messages

 Consumerism

 Drinking, drugs, & smoking

Director: Amy Heckerling
Cast: Alicia Silverstone, Brittany Murphy, Paul Rudd
Running time: 97 minutes
Release year: 1995
Genre: Comedy
MPAA rating: PG-13

FAMILIES CAN TALK ABOUT ...

Why is this movie considered a teen classic? Is it still relevant? How would it be different if it was made today?

The Color Purple

Powerful tale of survival with wrenching scenes of abuse.

age 14+ ★★★★★

In this inspiring drama, Celie, a Southern woman, journeys from abuse to independence. The film deals with traumatic issues, including child abuse, sexual abuse, racism, and sexism and has complex African-American characters rarely seen in American movies. Based on Alice Walker's novel.

 Positive messages

 Positive role models

 Violence & scariness

 Sexy stuff

 Drinking, drugs, & smoking

Director: Steven Spielberg
Cast: Danny Glover, Oprah Winfrey, Whoopi Goldberg
Running time: 152 minutes
Release year: 1985
Genre: Drama
MPAA rating: PG-13

FAMILIES CAN TALK ABOUT ...

How have times changed since the era in which this story was set? Has anything remained the same?

Crouching Tiger, Hidden Dragon

Magical, award-winning martial-arts fairy tale.

 age 12+ ★★★★★

The passionately romantic story of two sets of star-crossed lovers who face enormous obstacles, within themselves and imposed by the outside world. With breathtaking landscapes, gorgeous costumes, magnificent cello music from Yo-Yo Ma, and the most brilliantly staged fight scenes ever put on film.

 Positive role models

 Violence & scariness

Director: Ang Lee
Cast: Chow Yun-Fat, Michelle Yeoh, Zhang Ziyi
Running time: 120 minutes
Release year: 2000
Genre: Action/Adventure
MPAA rating: PG-13

FAMILIES CAN TALK ABOUT ...

How have women historically been portrayed in martial-arts films and in action movies as a whole? How are women portrayed differently in this movie?

The Dark Crystal

A fantastic but more intense Muppet adventure.

 age 7+ ★★★★☆

In this Jim Henson puppet feature, a planet is ruled by cruel creatures, thanks to the power and longevity granted by the Dark Crystal. But a prophecy has warned of a Gelfing being able to end their reign, and young Jen is sent to fulfill it. Fantasy-loving kids will survive the scary parts.

 Positive messages

 Positive role models

 Violence & scariness

Director: Frank Oz
Cast: Dave Goelz, Frank Oz, Jim Henson
Running time: 93 minutes
Release year: 1982
Genre: Fantasy
MPAA rating: PG

FAMILIES CAN TALK ABOUT ...

How is this story a hero's journey? What other stories follow the same formula?

The Dark Knight

Excellent sequel much darker, more violent than the first.

 age 15+ ★★★★★

Big, bold, and bruising, this is a prime example of how a high-budget, high-profile comic-book sequel can still be an actual movie — well-made, exciting, invested, and engaging. Heath Ledger won the Academy Award for Best Supporting Actor as the nightmarish Joker in his final role before his death.

 Violence & scariness

Director: Christopher Nolan
Cast: Aaron Eckhart, Christian Bale, Heath Ledger
Running time: 152 minutes
Release year: 2008
Genre: Action/Adventure
MPAA rating: PG-13

FAMILIES CAN TALK ABOUT ...

What distinguishes Batman from the Joker? Both are angry and dark; why is one a hero and one a villain?

Dead Poets Society

Inspiring, intense story of a teacher and his students.

 age 13+ ★★★★☆

The boys at a prestigious prep school aren't prepared for the new English teacher, Mr. Keating (Robin Williams), who encourages them to think for themselves and "seize the day!" Older kids fall hard for this coming-of-age drama, which belongs to the ensemble cast of young male actors.

 Positive messages

 Violence & scariness

 Drinking, drugs, & smoking

Director: Peter Weir
Cast: Dylan Kussman, Ethan Hawke, Robin Williams
Running time: 128 minutes
Release year: 1989
Genre: Drama
MPAA rating: PG

FAMILIES CAN TALK ABOUT ...

Which movies inspire you? Why? What about teachers?

Do the Right Thing

Spike Lee's masterwork of racial unrest; discuss with kids.

 age 16+ ★★★★☆

On one hot summer day in the Bedford-Stuyvesant neighborhood of Brooklyn, residents battle despair, joblessness, discrimination, and each other. Blame is everywhere; anger predominates. Spike Lee's intense study of racism in urban America during the late 1980s.

 Violence & scariness

 Sexy stuff

#! Language

Director: Spike Lee
Cast: Danny Aiello, Ossie Davis, Spike Lee
Running time: 120 minutes
Release year: 1989
Genre: Drama
MPAA rating: R

FAMILIES CAN TALK ABOUT …

Why does the story take place over one day? How does the music represent the characters' view of the world?

Dr. Seuss' How the Grinch Stole Christmas

Heartwarming TV special true to Seuss' classic.

 age 4+ ★★★★★

It's the day before Christmas, and all the Grinch can think about is how much he hates the whole season — so he hatches a plot to stop it from coming. But can the love that Christmas embodies save his shriveled heart? This 30-minute cartoon is sweet and soothing, and kids will howl in delight.

⊕ Positive messages

Director: Chuck Jones
Cast: Boris Karloff
Running time: 26 minutes
Release year: 1966
Genre: Animation
MPAA rating: NR

FAMILIES CAN TALK ABOUT …

Would you enjoy Christmas as much without presents? How do you make Christmas special?

Dr. Strangelove: Or, How I Learned to Stop Worrying and Love the Bomb

Black-comedy Kubrick classic for smart teens+.

 age 14+ ★★★★★

American General Jack D. Ripper goes mad and sends planes to drop nuclear bombs on the Soviet Union. Officials scramble to deal with the situation, but can the attack be stopped in time? The blackest of black comedies, with a sophisticated mix of satire and politics. Teens will need some context.

⬤ Violence & scariness

Director: Stanley Kubrick
Cast: George C. Scott, Peter Sellers, Sterling Hayden
Running time: 95 minutes
Release year: 1964
Genre: Comedy
MPAA rating: NR

FAMILIES CAN TALK ABOUT ...

What do you think of making fun of issues like madness and nuclear war? If the movie were to be made today, what details would be changed?

Drumline

Outstanding cast, great message, strong language.

⬤ age 12+ ★★★★☆

John Philip Sousa never dreamed marching bands could be this cool. Here they're as soul-stirring as raise-the-roof gospel and more irresistibly foot-stompingly, hip-hoppily thrilling than any video on MTV. The story may be an old one, but the details of this unexplored world make it fresh.

 Positive messages

 Positive role models

 Language

Director: Charles Stone
Cast: Nick Cannon, Orlando Jones, Zoe Saldana
Running time: 118 minutes
Release year: 2002
Genre: Drama
MPAA rating: PG-13

FAMILIES CAN TALK ABOUT ...

What does "one band, one sound" mean? Why does Dr. Lee think that honor and discipline are more important than talent?

Duck Soup

Classic comedy film with lots of mayhem, slapstick humor.

 age 7+ ★★★★★

Banned by Mussolini, this film is considered a comedic masterwork. The Marx Brothers are the epitome of anarchy: rude, insulting, pranksterish, and loyal to no one. Laugh and enjoy — and if some of the military madness and government misfits remind you of today's leaders, discuss with the kids.

Director: Leo McCarey

Cast: Chico Marx, Groucho Marx, Harpo Marx, Margaret Dumont

Running time: 68 minutes

Release year: 1933

Genre: Comedy

MPAA rating: NR

FAMILIES CAN TALK ABOUT ...

When does the comedy of the Marx Brothers seem timeless, and when does it seem dated?

Edward Scissorhands

Dark yet sweet underdog tale for older kids.

 age 13+ ★★★★☆

A darkly sweet portrait of adolescent angst. Edward's social awkwardness and deer-in-headlights self-consciousness is adorable enough to soften the sharpest of his pointed appendages. Exposes the cynical underbelly of front-porch Americana, forcing us to find beauty and truth in the grotesque.

 Positive messages

 Positive role models

 Violence & scariness

Director: Tim Burton

Cast: Dianne Wiest, Johnny Depp, Winona Ryder

Running time: 100 minutes

Release year: 1990

Genre: Fantasy

MPAA rating: PG-13

FAMILIES CAN TALK ABOUT ...

What's "normal"? How does conformity play a role in the townspeople's treatment of Edward?

Elf

Peppy holiday favorite for both kids and parents.

 age 7+ ★★★★☆

Buddy has been raised as one of Santa's elves but discovers at age 30 that his real father lives in NYC. Buddy leaves the North Pole to find his dad, and his naive pleasure in the world is almost as endearing to us as it is to (almost) everyone he meets. Will Ferrell as Buddy is hilarious.

 Positive messages

 Positive role models

Director: Jon Favreau

Cast: James Caan, Mary Steenburgen, Will Ferrell, Zooey Deschanel

Running time: 90 minutes

Release year: 2003

Genre: Comedy

MPAA rating: PG

FAMILIES CAN TALK ABOUT ...

Are you more likely to laugh at Buddy or with him? Why? What's the difference?

E.T.: The Extra-Terrestrial

Spielberg's family classic is still one of the best.

 age 7+ ★★★★★

Young Elliott discovers an extra-terrestrial left behind by fellow aliens, and the two develop a close bond. But it becomes clear E.T. can't survive on Earth, so Elliott must get him home. E.T. is one of the most recognizable creatures in film history and was a cultural touchstone for a generation.

 Positive messages

 Positive role models

 Violence & scariness

 Language

Director: Steven Spielberg

Cast: Dee Wallace, Drew Barrymore, Henry Thomas

Running time: 115 minutes

Release year: 1982

Genre: Science Fiction

MPAA rating: PG

FAMILIES CAN TALK ABOUT ...

Why do you think Elliott and his siblings understand E.T. in a way the adults in the movie can't?

Fantasia

Breathtaking animation feat — with some creepy visuals.

 age 6+ ★★★★★

This early animated film is a historical experience. Much of the imagery continues to astonish, even when compared with modern, computer-enhanced extravaganzas. Remember: Numerous sequences combine ominous, dark music and violent, scary visuals, which could be frightening for some kids.

 Positive messages

Violence & scariness

Director: James Algar, Samuel Armstrong
Cast: Deems Taylor, Julietta Novis, Leopold Stokowski
Running time: 120 minutes
Release year: 1940
Genre: Animation
MPAA rating: G

FAMILIES CAN TALK ABOUT ...

How can you tell when something is made up? Can something be scary even if you know it's not real?

Ferris Bueller's Day Off

Despite language, iffy behavior, this is a comedy classic.

 age 12+ ★★★★★

Bueller wants a break from school. Faking illness, he ropes his friends into joining him, and they hit Chicago in a 1961 Ferrari convertible. Exuberant and stacked hopelessly in favor of its chatty title character, this film is the most enjoyable and smarmiest of the smart kids/dumb parents genre.

#! Language

Director: John Hughes
Cast: Alan Ruck, Jeffrey Jones, Matthew Broderick
Running time: 103 minutes
Release year: 1986
Genre: Comedy
MPAA rating: PG-13

FAMILIES CAN TALK ABOUT ...

The filmmakers justify Ferris' attitude as a healthy response to self-centered, dumb, and materialistic adults. Do you agree?

Fiddler on the Roof

Epic musical story of Jews facing religious persecution.

 age 10+ ★★★★★

This epic musical, which centers on a humble agrarian family, is both a boisterous, comic look at rural life in a Ukrainian village and a serious portrait of the sweeping, tragic changes the 1905 Russian Revolution forced on Russian Jews. Starts off as a joyous trifle, then delves into politics.

 Positive messages

 Positive role models

 Violence & scariness

Director: Norman Jewison
Cast: Leonard Frey, Molly Picon, Norman Crane
Running time: 186 minutes
Release year: 1971
Genre: Musical
MPAA rating: G

FAMILIES CAN TALK ABOUT ...

What are the big messages of this film? How are the movie's messages relevant to today's cultural and political issues?

Finding Nemo

Sweet father-son tale has some very scary moments.

 age 5+ ★★★★★

On a journey that introduces him to extraordinary characters and teaches him a great deal about the world and himself, Marlin must go to the end of the ocean to find his son, Nemo — captured by a deep-sea-diving dentist who collects fish for his aquarium — to bring him home. A visual Pixar feast.

 Positive messages

 Positive role models

 Violence & scariness

Director: Andrew Stanton, Lee Unkrich
Cast: Albert Brooks, Ellen DeGeneres, Willem Dafoe
Running time: 101 minutes
Release year: 2003
Genre: Animation
MPAA rating: G

FAMILIES CAN TALK ABOUT ...

What parts of the movie were scary? Did anything that you think was going to be scary turn out not to be so bad?

Fly Away Home

Thrilling, touching adventure for animal lovers.

 age 8+ ★★★★★

A 13-year-old New Zealand girl is sent to live with her father in Canada after her mother dies in a car crash. She becomes a "mother goose" to a gaggle of motherless goslings and, with her father, helps them fly south for the winter, thus beginning to heal. A thrilling adventure, exquisitely told.

 Positive messages

 Positive role models

Director: Carroll Ballard
Cast: Anna Paquin, Dana Delany, Jeff Daniels
Running time: 107 minutes
Release year: 1998
Genre: Drama
MPAA rating: PG

FAMILIES CAN TALK ABOUT ...

How does Amy's cause help her heal after her mother's death? Why is it so important to her to keep the geese wild and free?

Forrest Gump

Moving and wonderful, but parent preview a good idea.

 age 13+ ★★★★★

Epic in length and symbolic in treatment, the film never loses sight of its love story. The relationship between the childlike Forrest and the disillusioned Jenny is an allegory for America's loss of innocence from the 1950s to the 1980s, reflected by pop culture and socio-political events.

 Positive messages

 Violence & scariness

 Sexy stuff

 Language

 Drinking, drugs, & smoking

Director: Robert Zemeckis
Cast: Robin Wright Penn, Sally Field, Tom Hanks
Running time: 135 minutes
Release year: 1994
Genre: Drama
MPAA rating: PG-13

FAMILIES CAN TALK ABOUT ...

What would you say the movie's main message is? Are viewers meant to admire Forrest? To sympathize with him?

Frankenstein

Classic monster movie still electrifies.

 age 10+ ★★★★★

Although this classic monster movie is tame by today's standards, it does deal with issues of life and death and scientific ethics. Boris Karloff invites sympathy with his portrayal of a tragic, misunderstood being with the body and strength of an ogre but the mind and innocence of a child.

 Violence & scariness

Director: James Whale
Cast: Boris Karloff, Colin Clive, Mae Clarke
Running time: 71 minutes
Release year: 1931
Genre: Thriller
MPAA rating: NR

FAMILIES CAN TALK ABOUT ...

What makes a movie scary? Do you think modern horror films rely too much on gratuitous violence and gore?

Frozen

Wintry Disney musical is fabulous celebration of sisterhood.

 age 5+ ★★★★★

Orphaned princesses must find a way to survive in this Disney film that combines show-stopping musical numbers, empowering heroines who discover their inner strength, stunning animated visuals, and scene-stealing sidekicks. The sweet themes of sisterhood and self-identity make for a delightful tale.

 Positive messages

 Positive role models

 Violence & scariness

Director: Chris Buck, Jennifer Lee
Cast: Jonathan Groff, Josh Gad, Kristen Bell
Running time: 102 minutes
Release year: 2013
Genre: Animation
MPAA rating: PG

FAMILIES CAN TALK ABOUT ...

What do Anna and Elsa learn over the course of the movie? How can you apply these lessons to your own life?

Gandhi

Brilliant biopic engages, educates, and inspires.

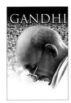

 age 12+ ★★★★★

Richard Attenborough's biopic spans Gandhi's adult life, showing how his spiritual principles of equality, tolerance, and nonviolence inspired India to push for independence from British rule. A must-see for families with an interest in history or civil rights. Ben Kingsley as Gandhi is brilliant.

 Positive messages

 Positive role models

 Violence & scariness

Director: Richard Attenborough
Cast: Ben Kingsley, Candice Bergen, Edward Fox
Running time: 190 minutes
Release year: 1982
Genre: Drama
MPAA rating: PG

FAMILIES CAN TALK ABOUT …

What motivated Gandhi, and why do you think people followed him? How was he a different kind of leader?

Ghostbusters

Paranormal '80s classic has some scares, innuendo.

 age 11+ ★★★★☆

The hilarious team of Bill Murray, Dan Aykroyd, and Harold Ramis fight ghosts in New York City. Eventually they must face off against apocalyptic forces, who've slipped in via Sigourney Weaver and Rick Moranis. The 1984 film combining comedy, action, and a little scary stuff stands up.

 Violence & scariness

 Sexy stuff

 Language

 Drinking, drugs, & smoking

Director: Ivan Reitman
Cast: Bill Murray, Dan Aykroyd, Harold Ramis, Sigourney Weaver
Running time: 107 minutes
Release year: 1984
Genre: Comedy
MPAA rating: PG

FAMILIES CAN TALK ABOUT …

What defines a hero? What other movies feature scientists and professors who save the day?

The Godfather

The classic tale of a Mafia family, violence and all.

✅ age 16+ ★★★★★

Mob-family patriarch Don Corleone is on his way out, and his most promising potential heir is his war-hero son, Michael. As family members cope with the trials of gangster life, the latent power structures of society and family become evident. Rightly considered one of the greatest films ever made.

 Violence & scariness

 Sexy stuff

 Drinking, drugs, & smoking

Director: Francis Ford Coppola
Cast: Al Pacino, James Caan, Marlon Brando
Running time: 175 minutes
Release year: 1972
Genre: Drama
MPAA rating: R

FAMILIES CAN TALK ABOUT ...

When, if ever, it is OK to operate outside of a corrupt legal system? Do the ends ever justify the means?

Goldfinger

Thrilling action comedy may be the best Bond.

✅ age 13+ ★★★★☆

James Bond is asked to monitor Auric Goldfinger, an international gold merchant the British government suspects to be plotting something vaguely fiendish. With an emphasis on gadgetry, womanizing, and humor in dire circumstances, this third installment is the template for all subsequent Bond films.

 Violence & scariness

 Sexy stuff

 Drinking, drugs, & smoking

Director: Guy Hamilton
Cast: Gert Frobe, Honor Blackman, Sean Connery
Running time: 110 minutes
Release year: 1964
Genre: Action/Adventure
MPAA rating: PG

FAMILIES CAN TALK ABOUT ...

Does 007's attitude toward women — often using them as pawns or treating them as pushovers — seem necessary to create his cool facade?

Gone with the Wind

Still one of Hollywood's best sweeping epics.

 age 10+

The four hours of this epic Civil War-era melodrama boast glamorous costumes, drama, violence, intrigue, sexism, and problematic depictions of slavery, as well as swoon-inducing romance between Scarlett O'Hara (Vivien Leigh) and Rhett Butler (Clark Gable). Winner of nine Oscars.

 Violence & scariness

 Sexy stuff

 Drinking, drugs, & smoking

Director: Victor Fleming
Cast: Clark Gable, Hattie McDaniel, Vivien Leigh
Running time: 238 minutes
Release year: 1939
Genre: Drama
MPAA rating: NR

FAMILIES CAN TALK ABOUT ...

How are African-Americans depicted in the movie? Do you think the portrayal of Civil War-era slavery would be different if this movie were remade today?

Good Will Hunting

Moving story of brilliant, troubled youth for older teens.

 age 15+

Will, a janitor at MIT, grew up as an abused foster child. When he solves math problems that stump the students, a professor seeks him out — and then seeks out an estranged friend (Robin Williams) to help him deal with Will. Gritty and moving, it's a powerful tale of realizing your potential.

 Positive messages

 Positive role models

 Language

 Drinking, drugs, & smoking

Director: Gus Van Sant
Cast: Ben Affleck, Matt Damon, Minnie Driver, Robin Williams
Running time: 126 minutes
Release year: 1999
Genre: Drama
MPAA rating: R

FAMILIES CAN TALK ABOUT ...

How do friends help and hinder each other in this movie? Do their relationships seem realistic?

The Goonies

A classic '80s action-fantasy — tweens will love!

 age 10+ ★★★★☆

A neighborhood in a Pacific Northwest coastal town is threatened with foreclosure and redevelopment when local kids find a map and clues to the loot of a 17th-century pirate chieftain — which could save their homes. Kids will love this rambunctious, pirate-themed treasure-hunt action-fantasy.

 Positive messages

 Violence & scariness

 Language

Director: Richard Donner
Cast: Corey Feldman, Josh Brolin, Sean Astin
Running time: 114 minutes
Release year: 1985
Genre: Action/Adventure
MPAA rating: PG

FAMILIES CAN TALK ABOUT ...
What kind of bond do these friends have? Are the characters relatable?

The Graduate

Influential coming-of-age sex comedy.

 age 15+ ★★★★★

This unique comedy charts an affair between a young man and a married friend of his parents — which lasts until he becomes interested in her daughter. Starring Dustin Hoffman and Anne Bancroft, this is a document of an era with a lush soundtrack by Simon and Garfunkel.

 Sexy stuff

Director: Mike Nichols
Cast: Anne Bancroft, Dustin Hoffman, Katharine Ross
Running time: 105 minutes
Release year: 1967
Genre: Comedy
MPAA rating: PG

FAMILIES CAN TALK ABOUT ...
Does Benjamin's lack of direction upon graduating seem applicable today, or is it more reflective of the state of youth in the '60s?

Grease

Musical phenomenon is great fun but a bit racy.

 age 12+ ★★★★☆

Don't expect a highly accurate portrayal of life in the 1950s, but the relationships will feel like familiar emotional ground. So will quintessential high school moments: the big pep rally, the school dance, worrying about image, and, of course, falling in love. And, boy, can John Travolta dance!

 Language

 Consumerism

 Drinking, drugs, & smoking

Director: Ken Annakin

Cast: John Travolta, Olivia Newton-John, Stockard Channing

Running time: 110 minutes

Release year: 1978

Genre: Musical

MPAA rating: PG

FAMILIES CAN TALK ABOUT ...

Do the movie's themes still resonate today, or do they feel dated? If you could update or remake this movie, how would you do it?

Groundhog Day

'90s comedy offers witty, sarcastic take on redemption.

 age 11+ ★★★★★

A cranky TV broadcaster is sent to capture a Groundhog Day celebration, but a snowstorm strands him in the town, and when he wakes up the next morning ... it's still Groundhog Day. Bill Murray shines in this uncommonly sweet comedy that delivers lots of laughs and some honest sentiment.

 Positive messages

 Positive role models

 Sexy stuff

 Drinking, drugs, & smoking

Director: Harold Ramis

Cast: Andie MacDowell, Bill Murray, Chris Elliott

Running time: 101 minutes

Release year: 1993

Genre: Comedy

MPAA rating: PG-13

FAMILIES CAN TALK ABOUT ...

What does Phil learn over the course of the movie? How long do you think it takes him to change his ways?

A Hard Day's Night

Beatles classic is Fab-ulous, but expect lots of smoking.

 age 8+ ★★★★★

A great intro to the Beatles, this surrealistic day-in-the-life "documentary" follows the most overwhelmingly popular rock group of all time through a typical 36 hours as they ostensibly try to get to the big show on time. Along the way are gags, character vignettes, and musical set pieces.

 Drinking, drugs, & smoking

Director: Richard Lester
Cast: George Harrison, John Lennon, Paul McCartney, Ringo Starr
Running time: 87 minutes
Release year: 1964
Genre: Musical
MPAA rating: G

FAMILIES CAN TALK ABOUT ...
Are there stars or artists who draw the same extreme reaction from fans today? How has the Internet changed how fans react and communicate with their idols?

Harry Potter and the Sorcerer's Stone

First Potter movie is a magical ride but also intense.

 age 7+ ★★★★★

On his 11th birthday, Harry receives a mysterious letter from Hogwarts, a boarding school for young witches and wizards, where he's expected in the fall. School begins; Harry meets his future best friends, Ron and Hermione; and things get exciting. Truly magical. The first movie in the series.

 Positive messages

 Positive role models

 Violence & scariness

Director: Chris Columbus
Cast: Daniel Radcliffe, Emma Watson, Rupert Grint
Running time: 152 minutes
Release year: 2001
Genre: Fantasy
MPAA rating: PG

FAMILIES CAN TALK ABOUT ...
Do you like the Harry Potter books or movies better? Which themes from the first story in the series pop up again in later installments?

High School Musical

A modern-day *Grease* for tweens.

 age 8+ ★★★★☆

This upbeat, made-for-TV movie is about a pair of teens who, after discovering a mutual love of song, overcome peer pressure to continue their newfound hobby. Zac Efron and Vanessa Hudgens give lively performances; both come across as friendly, well-adjusted, and immensely likable.

 Positive messages

 Positive role models

Director: Kenny Ortega
Cast: Ashley Tisdale, Vanessa Hudgens, Zac Efron
Running time: 98 minutes
Release year: 2006
Genre: Musical
MPAA rating: NR

FAMILIES CAN TALK ABOUT ...

How can teens stand up to friends who belittle their choices or talents?

Home Alone

Slapstick family holiday comedy brings the pain.

 age 7+ ★★★★☆

A mischievous 8-year-old gets left behind when his family leaves for a Christmas vacation in Paris. Kevin is elated — but soon realizes being home alone isn't all it's cracked up to be, especially when two bumbling burglars show up. The sweet story and great acting make this a holiday standout.

 Violence & scariness

 Language

Director: Chris Columbus
Cast: Daniel Stern, Joe Pesci, Macaulay Culkin
Running time: 103 minutes
Release year: 1990
Genre: Comedy
MPAA rating: PG

FAMILIES CAN TALK ABOUT ...

Do you think slapstick violence is funny? Is it ever OK to laugh when someone gets hurt?

Homeward Bound: The Incredible Journey

Adventurous animal tale will have kids riveted.

 age 6+ ★★★★☆

When their owners go on vacation, dogs Shadow and Chance and cat Sassy are left with a friend. Chance becomes convinced something's wrong and runs away; Sassy and Shadow follow. They have adventures, sharing wisecracks all the way, and finally arrive back home. Witty dialogue and well-cast voices.

 Positive messages

 Positive role models

Director: Duwayne Dunham
Cast: Don Ameche, Michael J. Fox, Sally Field
Running time: 84 minutes
Release year: 1993
Genre: Action/Adventure
MPAA rating: G

FAMILIES CAN TALK ABOUT ...

How did Shadow, Chance, and Sassy cope with their fear of being alone? How did working together make them stronger?

Hoop Dreams

Stunning documentary, great for older kids.

 age 13+ ★★★★★

This documentary follows two basketball standouts from Chicago from the eighth through the 12th grades as they aspire to the NBA. A searing portrait of inner-city life in America and the extraordinary, downright unfair expectations placed on the shoulders of many young black athletes.

 Positive messages

 Positive role models

 Language

 Drinking, drugs, & smoking

Director: Steve James
Cast: Arthur Agee, Emma Gates, William Gates
Running time: 171 minutes
Release year: 1994
Genre: Documentary
MPAA rating: PG-13

FAMILIES CAN TALK ABOUT ...

Do you think the media glamorizes professional sports and sports stars? If so, is that a positive or negative thing?

Hoosiers

Stirring tale of heroic sportsmanship will inspire families.

 age 9+ ★★★★★

A stirring movie about teamwork, discipline, and second chances that features exciting basketball action and a meticulous recreation of 1950s Indiana. Gene Hackman and Dennis Hopper are a high school coach and assistant coach, surprising everyone by bringing the team all the way to the state finals.

⊕ Positive messages

👥 Positive role models

🚭 Drinking, drugs, & smoking

Director: David Anspaugh
Cast: Barbara Hershey, Dennis Hopper, Gene Hackman
Running time: 114 minutes
Release year: 1986
Genre: Drama
MPAA rating: PG

FAMILIES CAN TALK ABOUT ...

How does the team manage to beat such seemingly insurmountable odds? Which qualities do the teammates share?

How to Train Your Dragon

Thrilling 3-D adventure sends brains-over-brawn message.

 age 7+ ★★★★☆

This high-flying adventure comedy mixes potentially frightening fantasy violence (and scary animated dragons) with a surprisingly touching story about the pressure of living up to your father's expectations, self-identity, growing up, and other seemingly heavy themes that are seamlessly woven into a funny, gripping tale. (And the sequel's great, too!)

⊕ Positive messages

👥 Positive role models

💥 Violence & scariness

Director: Chris Sanders, Dean DeBlois
Cast: America Ferrera, Craig Ferguson, Gerard Butler, Jay Baruchel
Running time: 90 minutes
Release year: 2010
Genre: Animation
MPAA rating: PG

FAMILIES CAN TALK ABOUT ...

Every hero on a journey has some help. Who helps Hiccup? Does he have any mentors or teachers? What about his friends?

Howl's Moving Castle

Charming Miyazaki fairy tale with surreal villains.

 age 8+

Keeping track of who's cursed whom and who's disguised as what can be confusing, but the major forces are clear: the war-making king vs. the well-meaning but petulant Howl. This Japanese animation investigates questions such as, Why do adults go to war? How is love scary and encouraging?

 Positive messages

 Positive role models

 Violence & scariness

Director: Hayao Miyazaki

Cast: Christian Bale, Emily Mortimer, Lauren Bacall

Running time: 119 minutes

Release year: 2005

Genre: Animation

MPAA rating: PG

FAMILIES CAN TALK ABOUT ...

How does the movie treat being old? When Sophie was put under a spell, how did she react to her new appearance?

Hugo

Spectacular book adaptation is great for tweens and up.

 age 8+

Twelve-year-old orphan Hugo lives in a Paris train station. He steals from shops to get by, but when he tries to swipe a wind-up mouse, he embarks on an adventure that leads him to learn about an automaton his dead father left him and why it's important. A spectacular film from Martin Scorsese.

 Positive messages

 Positive role models

Director: Martin Scorsese

Cast: Asa Butterfield, Chloe Grace Moretz, Christopher Lee

Running time: 127 minutes

Release year: 2011

Genre: Drama

MPAA rating: PG

FAMILIES CAN TALK ABOUT ...

What is the role of movies — to entertain, to educate, to provide meaning? Do all movies fulfill that role or only some?

The Hunger Games

Intense adaptation is violent, thought-provoking for teens.

 age 14+ ★★★★★

Every year, in a postapocalyptic future, a boy and a girl are randomly selected to compete in the Hunger Games, a televised battle to the death for the Capitol's amusement ... and as a brutal reminder of the 12 districts' failed rebellion. Violent, but in a heartbreaking way.

 Positive messages

 Positive role models

 Violence & scariness

Director: Gary Ross

Cast: Jennifer Lawrence, Josh Hutcherson, Liam Hemsworth, Woody Harrelson

Running time: 142 minutes

Release year: 2012

Genre: Action/Adventure

MPAA rating: PG-13

FAMILIES CAN TALK ABOUT ...

Why do you think there are more bleak portrayals of the distant future than optimistic ones? What are some other books and movies that feature a postapocalyptic or post-war future?

The Incredibles

Top-notch, action-packed fun for the entire family.

 age 7+ ★★★★★

Everyday life is challenging for superhero family the Incredibles, and this animated Pixar film is considered one of their best for portraying mature themes in a way kids and adults can enjoy. The human characters are vivid, believable, and utterly endearing, and the film is hilarious at every level.

 Positive messages

 Positive role models

 Violence & scariness

Director: Brad Bird

Cast: Craig T. Nelson, Holly Hunter, Samuel L. Jackson

Running time: 105 minutes

Release year: 2004

Genre: Animation

MPAA rating: PG

FAMILIES CAN TALK ABOUT ...

How does each member of the family help the others? Why are differences as important as similarities?

The Indian in the Cupboard

Classic, heartwarming fantasy will rivet kids.

 age 7+ ★★★★★

In this tender and compelling fantasy about friendship and compassion, a young boy receives a magical cupboard and a key that bring to life an 18th-century Iroquois warrior who's all of three inches tall. Tweens will enjoy the story, as well as the technical wizardry of Industrial Light and Magic.

 Positive messages

 Positive role models

 Language

Director: Frank Oz
Cast: Hal Scardino, Richard Jenkins, Steve Coogan
Running time: 97 minutes
Release year: 1995
Genre: Fantasy
MPAA rating: PG

FAMILIES CAN TALK ABOUT ...

What have you had to give up as you've grown up? How did Omri deal with the loss of his friends?

Indiana Jones and the Raiders of the Lost Ark

Indy's first adventure is a rip-roaring action masterpiece.

 age 11+ ★★★★★

Indy is in a race against the Nazis to find the secret resting place of the Ark of the Covenant, which contains the remnants of the Ten Commandments. Steven Spielberg and George Lucas forged a masterwork, and Harrison Ford proved himself to be one of the greatest all-time action-adventure heroes.

 Positive messages

 Positive role models

 Violence & scariness

 Language

 Drinking, drugs, & smoking

Director: Steven Spielberg
Cast: Harrison Ford, Karen Allen, Paul Freeman
Running time: 115 minutes
Release year: 1981
Genre: Action/Adventure
MPAA rating: PG

FAMILIES CAN TALK ABOUT ...

If Indy's a good guy, why does he break the rules? Is that OK? What separates him from the "bad" guys?

Inside Out

Beautiful, original story about handling big feelings.

 age 6+ ★★★★★

Creative, clever, heartfelt, and beautifully animated, this outstandingly original story about growing up has important messages about needing to feel — and express — all of your emotions, whether they're happy or sad.

 Positive messages

Positive role models

Director: Pete Docter
Cast: Amy Poehler, Phyllis Smith, Richard Kind
Running time: 102 minutes
Release year: 2015
Genre: Animation
MPAA rating: PG

FAMILIES CAN TALK ABOUT ...

What does it mean to have "mixed emotions" about something? Can you have joy without sadness? Why is it important to feel a range of emotions?

The Iron Giant

Touching robot-kid friendship tale with great messages.

 age 6+ ★★★★

Nine-year-old Hogarth Hughes lives with his waitress mother in rural Maine. One night, he discovers a huge robot, who turns out to be the world's best playmate. This wonderful film, set in the late 1950s, has so much humor and heart that it's one of the best family movies around.

 Positive messages

 Positive role models

 Violence & scariness

Director: Brad Bird
Cast: Cloris Leachman, Harry Connick Jr., Jennifer Aniston, Vin Diesel
Running time: 86 minutes
Release year: 1999
Genre: Animation
MPAA rating: PG

FAMILIES CAN TALK ABOUT ...

What makes a real friendship? Do you have to have a lot in common with someone to be friends with them?

Iron Man

Great action, lots of style, some iffy stuff.

 age 13+

Billionaire Tony Stark is abducted in Afghanistan and grievously wounded by the very weapons his company manufactures. Back in America, he vows to set things right with the help of a high-tech exoskeleton. Robert Downey Jr. elevates this film; he's funny, human, heroic, and completely engaging.

 Violence & scariness

Director: Jon Favreau

Cast: Gwyneth Paltrow, Jeff Bridges, Robert Downey Jr.

Running time: 125 minutes

Release year: 2008

Genre: Action/Adventure

MPAA rating: PG-13

FAMILIES CAN TALK ABOUT ...

Can heroic characters still be flawed? Does that make them more heroic or less?

It's a Wonderful Life

This classic delivers warmth all year long.

 age 9+

George Bailey (Jimmy Stewart) is a man with big plans whose even bigger heart keeps him from leaving his hometown. When he wishes he were never born, an angel shows him the tremendous impact he's had on his community. Frank Capra's bittersweet, heartwarming movie is a Christmas classic.

 Positive messages

 Positive role models

 Violence & scariness

Director: Frank Capra

Cast: Donna Reed, James Stewart, Lionel Barrymore

Running time: 125 minutes

Release year: 1946

Genre: Drama

MPAA rating: NR

FAMILIES CAN TALK ABOUT ...

How does each member of your family enhances the others' lives? How can you show that every day?

James and the Giant Peach

Fabulous adaptation of Roald Dahl's classic book.

 age 7+

In this adaptation of Roald Dahl's classic story, young James loses his parents and is forced to live as a servant to abusive relatives. He spills some magical crocodile tongues on the roots of a peach tree, which soon grows a giant peach, and six insects inside it become James' family.

 Positive messages

 Positive role models

 Violence & scariness

Director: Henry Selick
Cast: David Thewlis, Richard Dreyfuss, Susan Sarandon
Running time: 79 minutes
Release year: 1996
Genre: Animation
MPAA rating: PG

FAMILIES CAN TALK ABOUT ...

What role does imagination play in James' story? How did imagination make him feel better? How do you use your imagination?

Juno

Brilliant teen-pregnancy comedy, but iffy for kids.

 age 14+

This well-written, warmhearted comedy tackles a serious subject: teen pregnancy. Ellen Page plays the smart and soulful, warm and witty maverick Juno who's so unlike many of her peers and yet very much like them, too. Refreshing amid many other movies' disinterested, disaffected teens.

 Sexy stuff

 Language

Director: Jason Reitman
Cast: Ellen Page, Jason Bateman, Michael Cera
Running time: 92 minutes
Release year: 2007
Genre: Comedy
MPAA rating: PG-13

FAMILIES CAN TALK ABOUT ...

Does Juno's journey seem realistic? Do you think things would be likely to work out similarly in real life?

Jurassic Park

Terrifyingly realistic dinos run amok in sci-fi landmark.

 age 12+ ★★★★☆

On a secluded island, three scientists discover a jungle paradise where dinosaurs walk the Earth. Then a tropical storm strikes, and a corrupt computer programmer shuts down crucial security systems. Oscar-winning special effects, lots of frightful moments, and some good laughs.

 Positive messages

 Positive role models

 Violence & scariness

 Language

Director: Steven Spielberg
Cast: Jeff Goldblum, Laura Dern, Sam Neill
Running time: 127 minutes
Release year: 1993
Genre: Action/Adventure
MPAA rating: PG-13

FAMILIES CAN TALK ABOUT ...

What makes this movie scary? What's the difference between horror and suspense? Which has more impact on you, and why?

The Karate Kid

'80s classic is still fun for families with older tweens.

 age 11+ ★★★★☆

This 1980s cultural phenomenon has soul thanks to the teacher-student relationship between wise Mr. Miyagi (Pat Morita) and lonely teen Daniel (Ralph Macchio). Issues of class, race, (teen) romance, and even war are explored in the coming-of-age tale, where karate is a metaphor for life.

 Positive messages

 Positive role models

 Violence & scariness

 Language

Director: John G. Avildsen
Cast: Elisabeth Shue, Pat Morita, Ralph Macchio
Running time: 127 minutes
Release year: 1984
Genre: Drama
MPAA rating: PG

FAMILIES CAN TALK ABOUT ...

What other movies fit into the "underdog" genre? What are some similarities between the main characters' journeys?

The King's Speech

Superb drama about overcoming fears is fine for teens.

 age 14+ ★★★★★

In 1936, King George VI inherits the British throne — but he stammers. Over time, a speech therapist helps him gain the confidence and will to overcome his fears and let his voice be heard. Based on true events, with masterful performances from Colin Firth, Geoffrey Rush, and Helena Bonham Carter.

 Positive messages

 Positive role models

 Language

Director: Tom Hooper
Cast: Colin Firth, Geoffrey Rush, Helena Bonham Carter
Running time: 111 minutes
Release year: 2010
Genre: Drama
MPAA rating: R

FAMILIES CAN TALK ABOUT ...

Do you think the movie portrays the characters accurately? Why might filmmakers change some details in a fact-based story?

Lady and the Tramp

Classic Disney dogs paw their way into hearts of all ages.

 age 5+ ★★★★★

Lady is a pampered cocker spaniel who meets Tramp, a mutt from the other side of the tracks. With memorable songs and sweet characters, this classic taps into issues that will resonate with kids (like being neglected after a new baby arrives) as well as tropes (love across class lines).

 Positive messages

 Positive role models

Director: Clyde Geronimi, Hamilton Luske, Wilfred Jackson
Cast: Barbara Luddy, Larry Roberts, Peggy Lee
Running time: 76 minutes
Release year: 1955
Genre: Animation
MPAA rating: G

FAMILIES CAN TALK ABOUT ...

What are the benefits of Lady and Tramp's different lifestyles? What do they learn from each other?

The Land Before Time

Baby dinosaur buddy flick that started the series.

 age 5+

Curious, level-headed, longneck dinosaur Littlefoot and his prehistoric pals return in this animated series that promotes strength of character, dependability, self-respect, and friendship. The lovable characters ably mix positive messages with adventurous spirits.

🗨️ **Positive messages**

👤 **Positive role models**

💣 **Violence & scariness**

Director: Don Bluth
Cast: Candace Hutson, Judith Barsi, Will Ryan
Running time: 70 minutes
Release year: 1988
Genre: Animation
MPAA rating: G

FAMILIES CAN TALK ABOUT ...

Why is friendship so important to the characters? How do they each contribute to their group?

A League of Their Own

Terrific tweens-and-up story of women's baseball.

 age 10+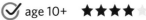

The all-star cast, including Geena Davis, Rosie O'Donnell, and Madonna, show the unique difficulties of the All-American Girls League in pre-feminist America, as well as the skills and friendships that develop among the Peaches. Tom Hanks is hilarious as the coach; the film is funny and poignant.

🗨️ **Positive messages**

👤 **Positive role models**

#! **Language**

🚬 **Drinking, drugs, & smoking**

Director: Penny Marshall
Cast: Geena Davis, Madonna, Tom Hanks
Running time: 124 minutes
Release year: 1992
Genre: Comedy
MPAA rating: PG

FAMILIES CAN TALK ABOUT ...

Do you think women could compete equally on men's sports teams? Why, or why not? What makes these characters role models?

The Lego Movie

Hilarious toy tale plugs product but is nonstop fun.

✓ age 6+ ★★★★☆

It's a testament to this film's team of veteran animation filmmakers that it's so smart, humorous, and visually fun to watch. Plus, there are real messages and sophisticated criticisms of popular culture and consumerism (pretty subversive — or very, very smart — for a movie tied to a multibillion-dollar toy company).

💬 Positive messages

➕ Positive role models

💥 Violence & scariness

💲 Consumerism

Director: Christopher Miller, Phil Lord
Cast: Chris Pratt, Elizabeth Banks, Will Arnett
Running time: 100 minutes
Release year: 2014
Genre: Animation
MPAA rating: PG

FAMILIES CAN TALK ABOUT ...

How can we all apply Vitruvius' lesson that everyone is special if we believe in our own talents and abilities?

Lincoln

Outstanding drama about revered leader's political genius.

✓ age 13+ ★★★★★

A political drama about the passing of the 13th Amendment and the end of the Civil War. There's no better film about how even our greatest leaders had to make quid pro quo overtures across party lines to move forward. Eloquently scripted by Pulitzer Prize-winning playwright Tony Kushner.

💬 Positive messages

➕ Positive role models

💥 Violence & scariness

#! Language

Director: Steven Spielberg
Cast: Daniel Day-Lewis, Joseph Gordon-Levitt, Sally Field
Running time: 150 minutes
Release year: 2012
Genre: Drama
MPAA rating: PG-13

FAMILIES CAN TALK ABOUT ...

How does the movie's depiction of President Lincoln compare to what you know or have learned about him? Did anything surprise you?

The Lion King

Musical king-of-the-beasts blockbuster is powerful, scary.

 age 6+ ★★★★☆

Considered one of Disney's greatest animated musicals, *The Lion King* does have some scary moments. But, despite a few sad sequences and a few evil characters, the overall message of Simba, the cub of Mufasa, the king of the jungle, is one of hope, love, and family responsibility

 Positive messages

 Positive role models

 Violence & scariness

Director: Rob Minkoff,Roger Allers
Cast: Ernie Sabella, Jeremy Irons, Matthew Broderick, Nathan Lane
Running time: 89 minutes
Release year: 1994
Genre: Animation
MPAA rating: G

FAMILIES CAN TALK ABOUT ...

What was the most disturbing part of the movie? How would the story be different without the intense moments?

The Little Mermaid

Superb, entertaining animated musical has some scary stuff.

 age 5+ ★★★★★

Ariel, a mermaid princess, rescues Prince Eric, thrown from his ship during a storm. Desperate to have a life with him, she makes an agreement with a sea witch — but will she be able to woo him in three days? A superbly entertaining musical based loosely on the fairy tale by Hans Christian Andersen.

 Positive role models

 Violence & scariness

Director: John Musker, Ron Clements
Cast: Christopher Daniel Barnes, Jodi Benson, Rene Auberjonois
Running time: 83 minutes
Release year: 1989
Genre: Animation
MPAA rating: G

FAMILIES CAN TALK ABOUT ...

How often do you see your favorite princesses on display when you're out shopping? Does watching their movies make you want to buy more of their stuff?

A Little Princess

Wonderful adaptation of classic book; some scary moments.

 age 7+ ★★★★

Sara is brought to a boarding school by her father, who's heading off to war. A remarkable, compassionate character, she sticks up for herself and all others and captivates the girls with her imaginative stories. A winning combination of magic, drama, boarding school bullies, and a resilient orphan.

 Positive messages

 Positive role models

Violence & scariness

Director: Alfonso Cuaron
Cast: Camilla Belle, Eleanor Bron, Liam Cunningham
Running time: 97 minutes
Release year: 1995
Genre: Fantasy
MPAA rating: G

FAMILIES CAN TALK ABOUT ...

Why are stories so important to Sara? How do they help her deal with her sadness?

Little Women (1949)

Adaptation of Alcott's story livened by superstar cast.

 age 9+ ★★★★

This 1949 adaptation of Louisa May Alcott's classic story of family love boasts a top-notch cast, including Elizabeth Taylor and Janet Leigh. Four sisters face deprivation and the absence of their father during the Civil War years, but they mature into accomplished young women.

 Positive messages

Positive role models

Director: Mervyn LeRoy
Cast: Elizabeth Taylor, Janet Leigh, June Allyson
Running time: 121 minutes
Release year: 1949
Genre: Drama
MPAA rating: NR

FAMILIES CAN TALK ABOUT ...

How is each of the March sisters unique? Do you and your siblings have complementary strengths?

The Lord of the Rings: The Fellowship of the Ring

Fabulous, but also violent and scary.

 age 12+ ★★★★★

Frodo Baggins is on a quest to return a powerful ring to the place where it was created so it can be destroyed — but he's in for some thrilling adventures. Peter Jackson's transcendent reminder of why we tell stories is astonishingly inventive; every detail is exactly, satisfyingly right.

➕ Positive messages

➕ Positive role models

💥 Violence & scariness

Director: Peter Jackson
Cast: Elijah Wood, Ian McKellen, Orlando Bloom
Running time: 208 minutes
Release year: 2001
Genre: Fantasy
MPAA rating: PG-13

FAMILIES CAN TALK ABOUT ...

If you were going to form a fellowship for a grand quest, who would you want to be in it? What would each member contribute?

Lucas

A realistic look at a teen's coming-of-age.

age 13+ ★★★★★

This quirky coming-of-age story centers on an "accelerated" 14-year-old boy who befriends newcomer Maggie. Viewers may cringe and even laugh at his antics, but they'll sympathize, too: No matter how clever Lucas is at covering the pain of being rejected, he's still an outsider who wants to fit in.

➕ Positive messages

➕ Positive role models

👄 Sexy stuff

#! Language

Director: George C. Seltzer
Cast: Charlie Sheen, Corey Haim, Jeremy Piven, Winona Ryder
Running time: 100 minutes
Release year: 1986
Genre: Drama
MPAA rating: PG-13

FAMILIES CAN TALK ABOUT ...

How is this movie similar to other coming-of-age tales? How is it different?

Mad Hot Ballroom

Enchanting dance documentary hits all the right beats.

 age 8+   ★★★★★

This documentary tracks students from three NYC public schools as they prepare for an annual citywide ballroom-dancing competition. The dedicated, enchanting fifth-graders learn the difficult steps and postures for the rumba, tango, swing, merengue, and fox trot — and learn much about themselves.

 Positive messages

 Positive role models

Director: Marilyn Agrelo
Cast: Emma Biegacki, Michael Vaccaro, Yomaira Reynoso
Running time: 105 minutes
Release year: 2005
Genre: Documentary
MPAA rating: PG

FAMILIES CAN TALK ABOUT ...

What do the kids in the movie gain from their experience? How do you cope with losing even when you try your best?

The Many Adventures of Winnie the Pooh

Remains faithful to A. A. Milne's beloved classic stories.

 age 3+   ★★★★★

This delightful animated tale brings to life several chapters of A.A. Milne's *The House at Pooh Corner*. With simple stories about childlike mishaps, this classic is visually and narratively appealing; the characters have varied personalities that demonstrate the rich variety one finds in real life.

 Positive messages

 Positive role models

Director: John Lounsbery, Wolfgang Reitherman
Cast: Paul Winchell, Sebastian Cabot, Sterling Holloway
Running time: 74 minutes
Release year: 1977
Genre: Animation
MPAA rating: G

FAMILIES CAN TALK ABOUT ...

All the animals have different personalities — can you describe them? Do you know any people with similar characteristics?

March of the Penguins

Stunning, loving documentary; some intense peril.

 age 6+ ★★★★★

Morgan Freeman narrates this documentary about the grueling annual trek made by Emperor penguins. They endure any number of hardships, and some die along the way, in their quest to mate, gestate, lay eggs, and protect them until the adorable fuzzy little hatchlings can walk home.

 Positive messages

 Violence & scariness

Director: Luc Jacquet
Cast: Morgan Freeman
Running time: 80 minutes
Release year: 2005
Genre: Documentary
MPAA rating: G

FAMILIES CAN TALK ABOUT ...

What role does the narration serve in playing up the movie's visual elements? How would it be different if there were no narration?

Mary Poppins

World's coolest nanny celebrates family and fun.

 age 6+ ★★★★★

In 1910, a British family seeks a new nanny for Jane and Michael. In flies magical Mary Poppins (Julie Andrews, in an Oscar-winning performance), not at all what Mr. Banks was looking for but precisely what the children ordered. Rare combo of fun with a simple, heartwarming story. Plus, the songs!

 Positive messages

 Positive role models

Director: Robert Stevenson
Cast: David Tomlinson, Dick Van Dyke, Julie Andrews
Running time: 140 minutes
Release year: 1964
Genre: Musical
MPAA rating: G

FAMILIES CAN TALK ABOUT ...

How does Mary Poppins get her messages across? What's easier to hear: a command or a song?

Matilda

Offbeat fantasy gem, but too dark for young kids.

 age 8+ ★★★★★

From the moment she's born, Matilda must learn to take care of herself. When her father finally allows her to go to school, it's a dream come true. The principal is a bully, but finally a teacher recognizes her exceptional abilities (including telekinesis). A fantasy based on the Roald Dahl book.

🔴 Violence & scariness

Director: Danny DeVito
Cast: Danny DeVito, Embeth Davidtz, Mara Wilson
Running time: 102 minutes
Release year: 1996
Genre: Fantasy
MPAA rating: PG

FAMILIES CAN TALK ABOUT …

What makes a movie a "good" or "bad" adaptation of a book?

Mean Girls

Mature but often-hilarious teen comedy.

 age 14+ ★★★★☆

Formerly homeschooled by her parents in Africa, Cady moves to Illinois for high school and finds herself drawn to the most popular clique. Her new friends appear sweet and supportive but are really competitive, duplicitous, and manipulative. Tina Fey wrote the screenplay and appears as a teacher.

➕ Positive messages

🔵 Drinking, drugs, & smoking

Director: Mark Waters
Cast: Lindsay Lohan, Rachel McAdams, Tina Fey
Running time: 95 minutes
Release year: 2004
Genre: Comedy
MPAA rating: PG-13

FAMILIES CAN TALK ABOUT …

Do you know any "mean girls"? How do you deal with them?

Millions

A beautiful, rare family film that everyone can enjoy.

✓ age 10+ ★★★★★

After you cut through all the intellectual and emotional layers, the brilliant cinematography, and the humor and excitement, this is the story of a lonely, loving child trying to be good, to do what's right, and to connect with the world of spirit. It's not often a movie like this comes along.

 Positive messages

 Positive role models

 Sexy stuff

Director: Danny Boyle
Cast: Alex Etel, James Nesbitt, Lewis McGibbon
Running time: 98 minutes
Release year: 2005
Genre: Drama
MPAA rating: PG

FAMILIES CAN TALK ABOUT ...

Whom would you help if you had the resources to spend? How would you decide who's worthy of the money when so many are in need?

Miracle on 34th Street

Classic holiday movie for the whole family.

✓ age 6+ ★★★★☆

Doris hires a Santa Claus for the Macy's Thanksgiving Day Parade, but when he shows up drunk, she quickly substitutes Kris Kringle — and Doris' daughter Susan begins to believe he's real. A heartwarming story about the importance of childhood wonder, trust, and standing up for what you believe.

 Positive messages

 Positive role models

Director: George Seaton
Cast: Edmund Gwenn, Maureen O'Hara, Natalie Wood
Running time: 96 minutes
Release year: 1947
Genre: Comedy
MPAA rating: NR

FAMILIES CAN TALK ABOUT ...

Why do you think Doris doesn't want Susan to use her imagination? Why do Kris and Fred think it's important?

Modern Times

Families will cherish Chaplin's silent slapstick.

 age 6+ ★★★★★

In this silent film, Charlie Chaplin loses his job on an assembly line, and mayhem ensues. Kids will be entertained by sight gags and outrageous characters (Chaplin experiments with roller skates at a department store); grown-ups and teens will notice razor-sharp commentary about class differences.

 Positive messages

 Positive role models

Director: Charlie Chaplin

Cast: Charlie Chaplin, Henry Bergman, Paulette Goddard

Running time: 103 minutes

Release year: 1936

Genre: Comedy

MPAA rating: NR

FAMILIES CAN TALK ABOUT ...

In what ways is a silent film different from a "talkie" — besides the fact that it's silent?

Monsters, Inc.

Cute, kid-friendly monster movie; may scare sensitive kids.

 age 5+ ★★★★☆

Monsters are afraid of kids, but they need to collect kids' screams to fuel their world. Unfortunately, kids are getting so hard to scare that the monsters' world is suffering from rolling blackouts. This movie is utterly delightful, with a delicious mix of heart, humor, and technical wizardry.

 Positive messages

 Positive role models

 Violence & scariness

Director: Andrew Adamson

Cast: Billy Crystal, John Goodman, Mary Gibbs

Running time: 92 minutes

Release year: 2001

Genre: Animation

MPAA rating: G

FAMILIES CAN TALK ABOUT ...

What does Sulley learn about kids? How does he change the factory for the better in the end?

Monty Python and the Holy Grail

Nonstop hilarity for families; some bawdy humor, profanity.

 age 13+ ★★★★★

Three decades later, this film is every bit as hilarious. God wants Arthur and his men to find the holy grail, so off they go, facing killer rabbits, randy vestal virgins, and other silly characters on their not-so-epic quest. One of the all-time best comedies for families with older kids.

 Violence & scariness

 Sexy stuff

 Language

Director: Terry Gilliam, Terry Jones
Cast: Eric Idle, Graham Chapman, John Cleese
Running time: 91 minutes
Release year: 1975
Genre: Comedy
MPAA rating: PG

FAMILIES CAN TALK ABOUT ...

How does the movie find humor in the misery and suffering that occurred during the Middle Ages?

Moulin Rouge

Dazzling musical romance for teens.

 age 15+ ★★★★☆

Whether you find this modern musical moving or maddening, it is fascinating. In late-1800s Paris, heartbroken poet Christian pursues the mantra that the greatest thing you'll ever learn is to love and be loved in return. With kinetic camerawork, color-saturated tableaus, and lots and lots of music.

 Positive messages

 Sexy stuff

Director: Baz Luhrmann
Cast: Ewan McGregor, John Leguizamo, Nicole Kidman
Running time: 127 minutes
Release year: 2001
Genre: Musical
MPAA rating: PG-13

FAMILIES CAN TALK ABOUT ...

Why is Hollywood enamored of opposites-attract themes? Are Satine and Christian truly destined for each other?

Mrs. Doubtfire

You'll laugh, you'll cry. Best divorce movie.

 age 12+ ★★★★☆

When his wife files for divorce and gets custody of the kids, Daniel is devastated. Then he hears his wife is looking for a nanny/housekeeper, so he transforms himself into a matronly old woman: Mrs. Doubtfire. Robin Williams is hilarious in this film that's sensitive about real human problems.

 Positive messages

 Positive role models

 Language

Director: Chris Columbus
Cast: Pierce Brosnan, Robin Williams, Sally Field
Running time: 125 minutes
Release year: 1993
Genre: Comedy
MPAA rating: PG-13

FAMILIES CAN TALK ABOUT ...

How does divorce affect families? Do you think this movie deals with the topic realistically?

Mulan

Disneyfied but dignified tale of Chinese warrior.

 age 5+ ★★★★☆

This lush Disney film — with some frightening scenes — is based on the story of China's legendary girl warrior, who dresses like a man and heads off to war against the Huns. She struggles at first but becomes a brave and skilled fighter, finding new friends in unexpected places.

 Positive messages

 Positive role models

 Violence & scariness

Director: Barry Cook
Cast: B.D. Wong, Eddie Murphy, Harvey Fierstein, Ming-Na
Running time: 90 minutes
Release year: 1998
Genre: Animation
MPAA rating: G

FAMILIES CAN TALK ABOUT ...

Is Mulan a role model? How does she compare to Disney's other heroines?

The Muppet Movie

First Muppet movie is full of wonderful songs, plus guns.

 age 6+   ★★★★☆

Kermit heads for Hollywood with a menagerie of equally ambitious Muppets including Fozzie Bear, Dr. Teeth and the Electric Mayhem, and Miss Piggy. Jim Henson's debut Muppet film was a technological breakthrough — but the beauty is that the characters' magic, innocence, and sweetness hold up.

 Positive messages

 Positive role models

 Violence & scariness

Director: James Frawley

Cast: Frank Oz, Jim Henson, Milton Berle

Running time: 94 minutes

Release year: 1979

Genre: Comedy

MPAA rating: G

FAMILIES CAN TALK ABOUT ...

Why do you think this movie, which was made decades ago, endures? What gives it all-ages appeal?

The Music Man

Glorious production with gorgeous music, dancing.

 age 6+   ★★★★★

Trouble comes to River City when "Professor" Harold Hill arrives, posing as a salesman of band instruments and uniforms. He wants to scam the locals but falls in love with the librarian-slash-music-teacher. Impeccable production, with some of the most gorgeous music and dancing ever filmed.

 Positive messages

 Positive role models

Director: Morton Da Costa

Cast: Buddy Hackett, Robert Preston, Shirley Jones

Running time: 151 minutes

Release year: 1962

Genre: Musical

MPAA rating: NR

FAMILIES CAN TALK ABOUT ...

This was originally a hit Broadway musical. What do you think the challenges might be in translating a Broadway production to the screen?

My Fair Lady

Witty, stylish musical classic will entertain all ages.

 age 6+ ★★★★★

In 1912 London, linguistics professor Henry Higgins picks cockney street peddler Eliza (Audrey Hepburn) to reshape her into an aristocrat — but he has his work cut out for him. The witty songwriting, charismatic performances, and lush costumes and sets may help kids muscle past the three-hour mark.

 Positive messages

Director: George Cukor

Cast: Audrey Hepburn, Rex Harrison, Wilfrid Hyde-White

Running time: 172 minutes

Release year: 1964

Genre: Musical

MPAA rating: G

FAMILIES CAN TALK ABOUT ...

How is the concept of social class addressed in the movie? How have things changed since the time in which it was set?

My Neighbor Totoro

Beautifully animated fantasy about friendship fit for all.

 age 5+ ★★★★★

In this breakthrough anime film, Satsuki and Mei move to the countryside where their mother is hospitalized. One day, Mei meets a rabbit-like creature she calls "Totoro," who helps them through their difficult time. A true family film, with a leisurely paced story and lushly detailed visuals.

 Positive messages

 Positive role models

Director: Hayao Miyazaki

Cast: Dakota Fanning, Elle Fanning, Patrick Carroll

Running time: 86 minutes

Release year: 1988

Genre: Animation

MPAA rating: G

FAMILIES CAN TALK ABOUT ...

How do the girls deal with their mother's sickness? Does the mother's hospitalization affect the sisters differently?

The Namesake

Fabulous immigrant-family saga to see with teens.

 age 14+ ★★★★★

A heartfelt depiction of a Bengali-American family that addresses the complexity of being raised by immigrant parents. A sudden tragedy brings Gogol home, where he rediscovers the meaning of his name and begins a new life with a fiercely modern wife and a deeper appreciation for his parents.

 Positive messages

 Positive role models

 Sexy stuff

 Drinking, drugs, & smoking

Director: Mira Nair
Cast: Irrfan Khan, Jacinda Barrett, Kal Penn
Running time: 122 minutes
Release year: 2007
Genre: Drama
MPAA rating: PG-13

FAMILIES CAN TALK ABOUT ...

How would you characterize the way the American media treats other cultures? Do some groups get treated differently from others? Why?

Napoleon Dyamite

One-of-a-kind high school comedy for the family.

 age 11+ ★★★★☆

Napoleon Dynamite just can't catch a break — and he may be clueless, but he has a great heart. The deliriously specific detail, superb use of the Idaho setting, affection for its characters, unexpected developments, and genuine sweetness keep us laughing with Napoleon, not at him.

 Positive messages

 Positive role models

Director: Jared Hess
Cast: Efren Ramirez, John Gries, Jon Heder
Running time: 82 minutes
Release year: 2004
Genre: Comedy
MPAA rating: PG

FAMILIES CAN TALK ABOUT ...

How is life for the teens in the movie like — or not like — your own experiences?

National Velvet

Great family movie; even better for horse lovers.

 age 7+ ★★★★★

The young Velvet Brown (Elizabeth Taylor) bonds with Mi Taylor (Mickey Rooney) over a love of horses. Messages about dreams, risk, determination, and honesty, with two strong female role models who succeed in sports previously closed to women: long-distance swimming and British horse-jumping.

 Positive messages

 Positive role models

Director: Clarence Brown

Cast: Donald Crisp, Elizabeth Taylor, Mickey Rooney

Running time: 123 minutes

Release year: 1944

Genre: Drama

MPAA rating: G

FAMILIES CAN TALK ABOUT ...

Why didn't Velvet want to make movies or do any of the other things people asked her to do after she won? What are the benefits and drawbacks of being a celebrity?

Network

Biting '76 satire with a media-literacy lesson.

 age 16+ ★★★★★

When the anchorman of a TV network finds out he's being fired, he announces he'll kill himself during his last broadcast. Often said to be the movie that predicted "trash TV," it seems especially on-target about the idea of huge, anything-for-money corporations running the media. For mature teens.

 Violence & scariness

 Sexy stuff

 Language

 Drinking, drugs, & smoking

Director: Sidney Lumet

Cast: Faye Dunaway, Ned Beatty, Peter Finch, Robert Duvall, William Holden

Running time: 121 minutes

Release year: 1976

Genre: Drama

MPAA rating: R

FAMILIES CAN TALK ABOUT ...

The movie argues that TV is a horrible, destructive force; do you agree? Which of the film's predictions have come true?

The NeverEnding Story

Boy bibliophile becomes part of fantasy tale.

✓ age 8+ ★★★★☆

Young Bastian escapes his troubled life in a dusty old bookstore, becoming engrossed in a forbidden book in which boy warrior Atreyu seeks to save the land of Fantasia from being destroyed by mythical force the Nothing. Powerful message of daring to dream and soaring to new heights through books.

 Positive messages

 Positive role models

 Violence & scariness

Director: Wolfgang Petersen
Cast: Barret Oliver, Gerald McRaney, Noah Hathaway
Running time: 94 minutes
Release year: 1984
Genre: Fantasy
MPAA rating: PG

FAMILIES CAN TALK ABOUT ...

What's the value of reading books? How can they transport you into another world?

The Nightmare Before Christmas

Tim Burton magic with just a touch of scariness.

✓ age 7+ ★★★★★

This stop-motion animation is one of the great family films for all ages. Tim Burton's fantasy centers on Jack Skellington, the Pumpkin King, who decides he needs to bring Christmas to Halloweentown. He'll do just about anything, too — even kidnapping Santa. Utterly weird, totally enchanting.

 Positive messages

 Positive role models

 Violence & scariness

Director: Henry Selick
Cast: Catherine O'Hara, Danny Elfman, Paul Reubens
Running time: 76 minutes
Release year: 1993
Genre: Animation
MPAA rating: PG

FAMILIES CAN TALK ABOUT ...

Why did Jack's experiment fail? Is it fair to expect people who have done something the same way for a long time to change quickly?

North by Northwest

Witty Hitchcock thriller piles on suspense and innuendo.

 age 11+  ★★★★☆

In this Hitchcock classic, Cary Grant is superb as Roger Thornhill, an advertising executive who's mistaken for a spy named George Kaplan. When his life is turned upside down, he decides the only way to get his life back is to track down the real Kaplan. Light and comic even in the tensest scene.

 Positive messages

 Drinking, drugs, & smoking

Director: Alfred Hitchcock
Cast: Cary Grant, Eva Marie Saint, James Mason
Running time: 131 minutes
Release year: 1959
Genre: Thriller
MPAA rating: NR

FAMILIES CAN TALK ABOUT ...

What makes this film a classic? What are some techniques that director Alfred Hitchcock uses that you've seen used in other movies?

October Sky

Inspiring tale for older tweens and up.

 age 10+  ★★★★★

This true story of a boy from a small town who dreams of becoming a rocket scientist is one of the best family movies ever made. The triumph of the underdog is one of literature's most enduring themes, and it's never done better. The script, the production design, and the acting are all superb.

 Positive messages

 Positive role models

 Language

Director: Joe Johnston
Cast: Chris Cooper, Jake Gyllenhaal, Laura Dern
Running time: 108 minutes
Release year: 1999
Genre: Drama
MPAA rating: PG

FAMILIES CAN TALK ABOUT ...

How does the movie portray the way that "nerds" are treated in school? Do you think people are evaluated differently in school from how they are once they get out?

Old Yeller

Tearjerker is one of the best early Disney dramas.

✅ age 8+ ★★★★★

Classic 1950s tearjerker about the love between a frontier family and a dog, with a now-legendary climax that could be hard for kids. Still, it's a classic and an excellent way to begin a discussion about life and death. The father is a model of wisdom and patience who validates his son's feelings.

➕ Positive messages

➕ Positive role models

💥 Violence & scariness

Director: Robert Stevenson
Cast: Dorothy McGuire, Fess Parker, Jeff York
Running time: 84 minutes
Release year: 1957
Genre: Drama
MPAA rating: G

FAMILIES CAN TALK ABOUT ...

How does Travis' attitude toward Old Yeller change throughout the movie? What do you think the movie's ultimate message is?

Oliver!

Glorious musical based on Dickens' *Oliver Twist*.

✅ age 8+ ★★★★☆

In this lavish musical adaptation, Oliver is booted from his orphanage; falls in with the Artful Dodger and Fagin's gang of pickpockets; sidesteps murderer Bill Sikes; and eventually is taken in by the wealthy Mr. Brownlow, who happens to be his uncle. Warm and memorable — and winner of six Oscars.

➕ Positive role models

💥 Violence & scariness

🚭 Drinking, drugs, & smoking

Director: Carol Reed
Cast: Mark Lester, Oliver Reed, Ron Moody
Running time: 153 minutes
Release year: 1968
Genre: Musical
MPAA rating: G

FAMILIES CAN TALK ABOUT ...

How does music help tell the movie's story? How would it be different without it?

The Parent Trap (1961)

Charming classic has some dated gender roles.

 age 6+ ★★★★

Sharon and Susan are as different as night and day and become enemies when they meet at summer camp. But when they discover they're identical twins, they switch places to try to reunite their parents so they can stay together. An entertaining relic from a time when kids were far less knowing.

 Positive messages

Director: David Swift

Cast: Brian Keith, Hayley Mills, Maureen O'Hara

Running time: 124 minutes

Release year: 1961

Genre: Comedy

MPAA rating: G

FAMILIES CAN TALK ABOUT ...

How are issues like divorce, sex, and puberty addressed here? How might that compare to a modern movie focused on tween characters?

Pee-Wee's Big Adventure

Just as charming and curious as it was in 1985.

 age 7+ ★★★★

When someone steals his bicycle, sprightly man-boy Pee-wee Herman embarks on the adventure of a lifetime in Tim Burton's madcap comedy. This quirky film is a cult classic among devotees of Paul Reubens' bow-tied alter ego, with wild production designs, some Claymation, and lots of unusual toys.

 Violence & scariness

Director: Tim Burton

Cast: Elizabeth Daily, Mark Holton, Paul Reubens

Running time: 90 minutes

Release year: 1985

Genre: Comedy

MPAA rating: PG

FAMILIES CAN TALK ABOUT ...

What makes Pee-wee such an entertaining character? Can you think of other characters who are as well-loved by many groups?

The Pianist

True story of a Jewish pianist; OK for older kids.

 age 16+ ★★★★★

The devastating true story of Wladyslaw Szpilman, a Jewish pianist in Poland caught in the horrors of World War II. Roman Polanski, a Holocaust survivor who lost many family members, powerfully conveys the journey of a man transformed from a highly cultured musician to a scavenging, debased shell.

 Positive messages

 Violence & scariness

Director: Roman Polanski
Cast: Adrien Brody, Emilia Fox, Thomas Kretschmann
Running time: 150 minutes
Release year: 2002
Genre: Drama
MPAA rating: R

FAMILIES CAN TALK ABOUT ...

Why might filmmakers sometimes tweak the facts in a movie based on a true story? How could you find out more about the actual events and people portrayed in the film?

Pinocchio

Disney masterpiece is darker than you may remember.

 age 6+ ★★★★★

Lonely woodcarver Geppetto wishes the wooden puppet he carved was a real boy. His wish is granted, but Pinocchio must become brave, truthful, and unselfish. This Disney classic passes the test of time for a beautiful and effective lesson on the perils of doing wrong when you should know better.

 Positive messages

 Positive role models

 Violence & scariness

 Drinking, drugs, & smoking

Director: Hamilton Luske
Cast: Cliff Edwards, Dickie Jones, Mel Blanc
Running time: 88 minutes
Release year: 1940
Genre: Animation
MPAA rating: G

FAMILIES CAN TALK ABOUT ...

What does it mean to "let your conscience be your guide"? How do you tell the difference between right and wrong, and what do you do if you can't figure it out?

Pirates of the Caribbean: The Curse of the Black Pearl

Rip-roaring fun for kids who don't mind skeletons.

 age 12+ ★★★★

A gold medallion is the missing piece to a treasure chest that once turned a boat of pirates into the undead. The delightfully convoluted plot involves swashbuckling romance, double-crossing, sea voyages, and plenty of pirate accents. Capt. Jack Sparrow (Johnny Depp) is undeniably fun to watch.

 Violence & scariness

 Sexy stuff

 Drinking, drugs, & smoking

Director: Gore Verbinski
Cast: Johnny Depp, Keira Knightley, Orlando Bloom
Running time: 135 minutes
Release year: 2003
Genre: Action/Adventure
MPAA rating: PG-13

FAMILIES CAN TALK ABOUT ...

Why is Captain Jack Sparrow such an appealing character? Is he a role model in any way? Why do we like him anyway?

Pride & Prejudice

Gorgeous Jane Austen adaptation has timeless appeal.

 age 11+ ★★★★

This BBC adaptation of Jane Austen's novel offers a long, hard look at the hypocrisy and bad manners of the English aristocracy as the Bennett sisters look for love among the wealthy. The acting is superb, and the story — as gripping as it is meaningful — has many comic moments.

 Positive messages

 Positive role models

Director: Joe Wright
Cast: Donald Sutherland, Keira Knightley, Matthew Macfadyen
Running time: 127 minutes
Release year: 2005
Genre: Romance
MPAA rating: PG

FAMILIES CAN TALK ABOUT ...

How are attitudes concerning love, gender roles, and economic class shown in the movie? How are things different today?

The Princess Bride

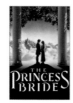

Witty, winsome fairy tale for the whole family.

 age 8+ ★★★★★

This film serves up every element of a classic romantic adventure — princes, villains, evil geniuses, giants, swordfights, revenge, kidnapping, and a rescue on white horses — with delicious humor. The storybook characters are consistently hilarious, and the film is resoundingly satisfying.

 Positive messages

 Positive role models

 Violence & scariness

Director: Rob Reiner

Cast: Cary Elwes, Mandy Patinkin, Robin Wright Penn

Running time: 98 minutes

Release year: 1987

Genre: Comedy

MPAA rating: PG

FAMILIES CAN TALK ABOUT ...

How does this movie poke fun at some of the standard fairy-tale elements?

The Princess Diaries

Sweet tale about growing up is terrific fun for families.

 age 8+ ★★★★★

Mia is a shy 15-year-old who'd like to kiss the class hunk and speak in class without fainting. Then her grandmother shows up to reveal ... she's a princess! Now Mia has to learn courage. A family movie in the best sense, with a wonderful story about growing up, finding yourself, and taking chances.

 Positive messages

 Positive role models

Director: Garry Marshall

Cast: Anne Hathaway, Hector Elizondo, Julie Andrews

Running time: 115 minutes

Release year: 2001

Genre: Comedy

MPAA rating: G

FAMILIES CAN TALK ABOUT ...

How does this movie address verbal bullying? Does it seem accurate or overblown? Why?

Psycho

Horror masterpiece definitely isn't for young kids.

 age 15+ ★★★★★

Marion steals money and skips town, then stops at a remote motel, run by Norman, who's cheerful but nervous. He mentions his overbearing, yet absent, mother. His hobby is taxidermy, and he happens to have the extra key to Marion's room ... One of the scariest movies ever made. A Hitchcock classic.

 Violence & scariness

Director: Alfred Hitchcock

Cast: Anthony Perkins, Janet Leigh, Vera Miles

Running time: 109 minutes

Release year: 1960

Genre: Thriller

MPAA rating: NR

FAMILIES CAN TALK ABOUT ...

A lot of the movie's violence is implied rather than shown. Is that scarier to you than graphic violence? Why, or why not?

Rashomon

Masterpiece about absolute truth. Best for teens.

 age 15+ ★★★★★

This psychologically and morally complex tale of a trial to determine who is at fault for a murder and possible rape works to expose the near impossibility of finding absolute truth in the world and the danger of condemning any one. The film that brought Akira Kurosawa to international renown.

 Violence & scariness

Director: Akira Kurosawa

Cast: Machiko Kyo, Masayuki Mori, Toshiro Mifune

Running time: 88 minutes

Release year: 1951

Genre: Drama

MPAA rating: NR

FAMILIES CAN TALK ABOUT ...

Have you ever been in a situation where you heard two different accounts of the same event? Which version did you believe? Why?

Real Women Have Curves

Ugly Betty star captivates in teen drama.

 age 14+ ★★★★★

The youngest daughter of an LA Mexican-American family wants to go to Columbia University. But her mother wants to marry her off so she can retire. A teen heroine movie that encourages girls to follow their dreams — and that shows a teenage girl who isn't white, rich, and pampered.

 Positive messages

 Positive role models

 Sexy stuff

 Language

Director: Patricia Cardoso

Cast: America Ferrera, Ingrid Oliu, Lupe Ontiveros

Running time: 85 minutes

Release year: 2002

Genre: Drama

MPAA rating: PG-13

FAMILIES CAN TALK ABOUT ...

Do you feel pressure to look a certain way? If so, where does that pressure come from?

Rebel Without a Cause

1950s James Dean teen-rage landmark still resonates.

 age 13+ ★★★★★

This landmark depiction of teen alienation and delinquency was an iconic screen drama of the 1950s, serious-minded and superbly acted. With James Dean, Sal Mineo, and Natalie Wood, it has plenty of don't-try-this-at-home moments, but in a Disney world *Rebel* remains forceful and un-phony.

 Drinking, drugs, & smoking

Director: Nicholas Ray

Cast: Dennis Hopper, James Dean, Natalie Wood

Running time: 111 minutes

Release year: 1955

Genre: Drama

MPAA rating: PG-13

FAMILIES CAN TALK ABOUT ...

Can today's teens still relate to Jim's anger, aggression, dysfunctional parents, and negative peer pressures?

The Red Balloon

Imaginative story told entirely through vivid visuals.

 age 7+ ★★★★★

This tender, enchanting, mostly silent short film about a red balloon that befriends a little French boy is a rare and invigorating pleasure. Winner of an Academy Award for Best Original Screenplay, the Cannes Grand Prize, and the 1968 Best Film of the Decade Educational Film Award.

 Positive role models

Director: Albert Lamorisse

Cast: Georges Sellier, Pascal Lamorisse, Paul Perey

Running time: 34 minutes

Release year: 1957

Genre: Drama

MPAA rating: NR

FAMILIES CAN TALK ABOUT ...

How is color used throughout the movie? How is color used in other movies?

Remember the Titans

Inspiring football drama brings history to life.

 age 10+  ★★★★☆

This movie about the real-life integration of a Virginia high school football team teeters on the brink of cliché and stereotype but manages to come down on the side of archetype, thanks to a sure script, solid direction, and a sensational performance by Denzel Washington as the coach.

 Positive messages

 Positive role models

Director: Boaz Yakin

Cast: Denzel Washington, Donald Faison, Will Patton

Running time: 113 minutes

Release year: 2000

Genre: Drama

MPAA rating: PG

FAMILIES CAN TALK ABOUT ...

Why are so many sports movies inspiring? What are some of your other favorites?

Roman Holiday

Delightful classic is perfect for family movie night.

 age 9+ ★★★★★

Audrey Hepburn (in her debut performance) plays a princess on the lam from her embassy and is discovered on a park bench by tall, dark, and handsome leading man Gregory Peck. The two spend the day playing hooky in Rome — what more could you ask for in a romance?

 Positive messages

 Positive role models

 Violence & scariness

Director: William Wyler

Cast: Audrey Hepburn, Eddie Albert, Gregory Peck

Running time: 118 minutes

Release year: 1953

Genre: Romance

MPAA rating: NR

FAMILIES CAN TALK ABOUT …

How do you think the movie would be different if it was remade today? How do the gender roles reflect the time in which it was made?

Rudy

Inspiring sports film about a real-life underdog.

 age 11+ ★★★★★

Rudy is a working-class kid for whom education is a hurdle that must be cleared to realize his dream to play football for Notre Dame. More than the wildest science-fiction or fantasy story, this film will make you believe anything — with perseverance and grueling hard work — is possible.

 Positive messages

 Positive role models

 Violence & scariness

#! Language

Director: David Anspaugh

Cast: Charles S. Dutton, Jon Favreau, Sean Astin

Running time: 112 minutes

Release year: 1993

Genre: Drama

MPAA rating: PG

FAMILIES CAN TALK ABOUT …

What's appealing about sports movies? What kinds of feelings do they stir up?

The Sandlot

Field of Dreams for tweens.

 age 8+

A sports film for kids that isn't about winning. After lucking onto the local sandlot team, Scotty spends a blissful summer honing his baseball skills with help from his teammates. When the gang experiences what they believe is a bad omen, they're off in search of a good one to counterbalance it.

 Positive messages

 Language

Director: David M. Evans

Cast: James Earl Jones, Mike Vitar, Tom Guiry

Running time: 101 minutes

Release year: 1993

Genre: Comedy

MPAA rating: PG

FAMILIES CAN TALK ABOUT ...

In sports movies, is it always a guarantee that the underdogs will come out on top?

Say Anything

A gem of a coming-of-age story.

 age 15+

A frank portrait of teens on the cusp of adulthood, this smart, funny movie based in Seattle mines a template for coming-of-age movies — and comes up with gold. Using stock elements of the genre — hip soundtrack, slacker kids, and screwed-up families — this is the stuff of great drama.

 Positive messages

 Positive role models

 Sexy stuff

 Language

Director: Cameron Crowe

Cast: Ione Skye, Joan Cusack, John Cusack

Running time: 100 minutes

Release year: 1989

Genre: Romance

MPAA rating: PG-13

FAMILIES CAN TALK ABOUT ...

Do you think this movie is still relevant? Why do you think it's considered a teen classic?

Schindler's List

Accurate, heartbreaking masterpiece about the Holocaust.

 age 15+ ★★★★★

This brutal, emotionally devastating, three-hour drama won several Oscars and has a powerful message about the human spirit — but pulls no punches in depicting WWII. Steven Spielberg is a virtuoso filmmaker here, searching for the one true story that will make the Holocaust comprehensible.

 Positive messages

 Positive role models

 Violence & scariness

 Sexy stuff

Director: Steven Spielberg
Cast: Ben Kingsley, Liam Neeson, Ralph Fiennes
Running time: 196 minutes
Release year: 1993
Genre: Drama
MPAA rating: R

FAMILIES CAN TALK ABOUT ...

How can individuals make a difference in even the most extreme or tragic circumstances?

School of Rock

Standout Jack Black in nerds-become-cool comedy.

 age 11+ ★★★★☆

Jack Black plays Dewey Finn, a musician who lives for rock. He's loud, immature, messy, and self-absorbed. But he fakes his way into a job as a fifth-grade substitute teacher at a prep school, where he and the kids learn something new. Black is enormously entertaining, and the kids are terrific.

 Positive messages

 Positive role models

 Language

Director: Richard Linklater
Cast: Jack Black, Joan Cusack, Mike White
Running time: 108 minutes
Release year: 2003
Genre: Comedy
MPAA rating: PG-13

FAMILIES CAN TALK ABOUT ...

What's the most important thing Dewey learns from the kids, and what is the most important thing they learn from him?

The Secret of NIMH

Fascinating, but very dark with some creepy imagery.

 age 8+ ★★★★

Forced to move from her home, widowed mouse Mrs. Brisby discovers an underground rat civilization; her late husband helped them escape experimentation and injection with intelligence drugs. The story's tone frequently careens from cheerfulness to grimness and is sometimes downright terrifying.

 Positive role models

 Violence & scariness

Director: Don Bluth

Cast: Derek Jacobi, Dom DeLuise, Elizabeth Hartman

Running time: 83 minutes

Release year: 1982

Genre: Animation

MPAA rating: G

FAMILIES CAN TALK ABOUT ...

Which parts of the movie were the scariest? Why? Would the movie have been more or less scary if it weren't animated?

Selena

Touching and ultimately tragic tale of young Tejano star.

 age 10+ ★★★★

A touching, effervescent, and ultimately tragic biopic about the Grammy-winning Tejano singer Selena (Jennifer Lopez), who in 1995, at age 23, was killed by her fan-club president. At the center is a portrait of a principled and loving Latino family — something rarely depicted in movies.

 Positive messages

 Positive role models

Director: Gregory Nava

Cast: Constance Marie, Edward James Olmos, Jennifer Lopez

Running time: 128 minutes

Release year: 1997

Genre: Drama

MPAA rating: PG

FAMILIES CAN TALK ABOUT ...

How does the movie depict Selena as a role model? How does she succeed despite ethnic and gender challenges?

Selma

Outstanding drama about MLK's fight for equal rights.

 age 13+ ★★★★★

This powerful, educational, well-acted drama — one of the finest films ever made about the civil rights movement — is a great choice for parents to watch with teens (and even mature tweens).

 Positive messages

 Positive role models

 Violence & scariness

 Language

Director: Ava DuVernay
Cast: David Oyelowo, Carmen Ejogo, Tim Roth
Running time: 122 minutes
Release year: 2014
Genre: Drama
MPAA rating: PG-13

FAMILIES CAN TALK ABOUT ...

How do the lessons from the civil rights movement apply today? Are people still discriminated against? How can that be remedied?

Sense and Sensibility

A lush and witty adaptation of Jane Austen's novel.

 age 11+ ★★★★★

Directed by Ang Lee, Emma Thompson's adaptation of the Jane Austen novel follows the Dashwood sisters as they try to redeem a lost fortune by marrying well and end up finding love. The loving depiction of the family as a high-spirited and supportive clan is positively endearing.

 Positive messages

 Positive role models

Director: Ang Lee
Cast: Alan Rickman, Emma Thompson, Kate Winslet
Running time: 136 minutes
Release year: 1995
Genre: Romance
MPAA rating: PG

FAMILIES CAN TALK ABOUT ...

How are the values of the time conveyed in this movie? How are they similar to and different from today's values, in terms of love, money, and family?

The Shawshank Redemption

Gritty but comforting story of friendship.

 age 15+ ★★★★☆

Andy is convicted of murder and sent to prison. He befriends Red and gets a job in the prison library. Things unravel, but there's a happy ending, and the valuable lesson of friendship between blacks and whites may inspire children who haven't heard the story a hundred times.

 Positive messages

 Positive role models

 Violence & scariness

#! Language

Director: Frank Darabont
Cast: Bob Gunton, Morgan Freeman, Tim Robbins
Running time: 142 minutes
Release year: 1994
Genre: Drama
MPAA rating: R

FAMILIES CAN TALK ABOUT ...

Why do you think Red and Andy disagreed on whether they should have hope for a better life? Did their class and race affect their approach?

Shrek

Gross-out laughs meet a marvelous fairy-tale mix.

 age 6+ ★★★★★

Shrek, a big, green ogre, lives happily alone in a swamp until Lord Farquaad sets out to get rid of all the fairy-tale characters and send them to "a designated resettlement community." Sensational animation, adventure, romance, laughter — and plenty of potty humor.

 Positive messages

 Positive role models

 Violence & scariness

#! Language

Director: Andrew Adamson, Vicky Jenson
Cast: Cameron Diaz, Eddie Murphy, Mike Myers
Running time: 93 minutes
Release year: 2001
Genre: Animation
MPAA rating: PG

FAMILIES CAN TALK ABOUT ...

What does it mean to say that ogres are like onions? How do people have layers?

Singin' in the Rain

Often considered the finest musical of all time.

 age 6+   ★★★★★

Widely considered to be the best Hollywood musical ever made, with one of the top 10 moments: Gene Kelly splashing and singing in the rain — a "glorious feeling" that's contagious. With classic numbers and a witty script that's unusually sharp and satiric for a musical comedy.

 Positive messages

Director: Stanley Donen
Cast: Debbie Reynolds, Donald O'Connor, Gene Kelly
Running time: 102 minutes
Release year: 1952
Genre: Musical
MPAA rating: NR

FAMILIES CAN TALK ABOUT ...

Discuss the history of movies and the period in which silent movies gave way to "talkies." What were some of the problems? What were some of the benefits?

The Sisterhood of the Traveling Pants

Sensitive portrayal of four girls' friendships.

 age 12+   ★★★★☆

Four high school girlfriends separate for the summer but vow to keep in touch by way of a pair of magic blue jeans that perfectly fits them all. At times sentimental but ultimately sensible, it's about learning to respect what's in front of you as well as new experiences. Strong female characters.

 Positive messages

 Positive role models

 Sexy stuff

Director: Ken Kwapis
Cast: Alexis Bledel, Amber Tamblyn, America Ferrera
Running time: 119 minutes
Release year: 2005
Genre: Drama
MPAA rating: PG

FAMILIES CAN TALK ABOUT ...

How can you be mad at someone but at the same time still love him or her? How can loss also be an occasion for learning, sharing, and emotional growth?

Sixteen Candles

Racy, drunken, hilarious '80s high school comedy.

 age 16+ ★★★★

In this hair-raising tour of adolescence, Sam is turning 16, but her family has forgotten her birthday. Director John Hughes recreates the little humiliations that can make teen life a living hell. An adult comedy with teen characters that has sharply observed moments and now-dated stereotypes.

 Sexy stuff

 Language

 Drinking, drugs, & smoking

Director: John Hughes
Cast: Anthony Michael Hall, Michael Schoeffling, Molly Ringwald
Running time: 93 minutes
Release year: 1984
Genre: Comedy
MPAA rating: PG

FAMILIES CAN TALK ABOUT ...

Discuss the stereotyped character of Long Duk Dong. How has that stereotype changed today?

The Sixth Sense

Great, but sometimes scarier than R-rated horror.

 age 14+ ★★★★

A thinking person's thriller, with one of the finest performances ever given by a child, Haley Joel Osment, who plays the patient of a child therapist (Bruce Willis). At times it's scarier than R-rated films, and viewers may find the thoughtful views on life and death comforting or disturbing.

 Positive role models

 Violence & scariness

Director: M. Night Shyamalan
Cast: Bruce Willis, Haley Joel Osment, Toni Collette
Running time: 106 minutes
Release year: 1999
Genre: Thriller
MPAA rating: PG-13

FAMILIES CAN TALK ABOUT ...

What makes this story particularly gripping? How does the director scare you without going for over-the-top violence?

Slumdog Millionaire

Epic romance-drama is brilliant but too mature for kids.

 age 16+ ★★★★★

Jamal has made it to the second-to-last question on a quiz show, and the cops want to know how he's cheating — the only way an uneducated boy from the slums could be winning. A big, bold, beautiful film about heroism, true love, and unfailing friendship set in rough-and-tumble modern India.

 Positive role models

 Violence & scariness

 Language

 Drinking, drugs, & smoking

Director: Danny Boyle
Cast: Dev Patel, Freida Pinto, Irrfan Khan
Running time: 120 minutes
Release year: 2008
Genre: Drama
MPAA rating: R

FAMILIES CAN TALK ABOUT ...
Discuss how the movie depicts the differences — and similarities — between Indian culture and American culture. How are they different? What do they have in common?

Snow White and the Seven Dwarfs

Animated classic is enchanting but also scary.

 age 5+ ★★★★☆

This classic was the first feature-length animated film in history. Girls nowadays like their princesses and movie idols with a little edge, but considering this was made in 1937, it's still timeless and chock-full of the key ingredients for a Disney success: romance, mystery, mild peril, and music.

 Positive messages

 Violence & scariness

Director: David Hand
Cast: Adriana Caselotti, Harry Stockwell, Lucille La Verne
Running time: 84 minutes
Release year: 1937
Genre: Animation
MPAA rating: G

FAMILIES CAN TALK ABOUT ...
Snow White is a traditional damsel in distress. How have depictions of princesses and heroines changed since 1937?

Some Like It Hot

One of the wildest romantic farces ever.

 age 11+ ★★★★★

This Billy Wilder classic follows Joe and Jerry, who flee (in drag) after accidentally witnessing the St. Valentine's Day Massacre. Brilliant performances by all three stars — Marilyn Monroe, Jack Lemmon, and Tony Curtis — give this film a lot of heart.

 Sexy stuff

 Drinking, drugs, & smoking

Director: Billy Wilder

Cast: Jack Lemmon, Marilyn Monroe, Tony Curtis

Running time: 121 minutes

Release year: 1959

Genre: Comedy

MPAA rating: NR

FAMILIES CAN TALK ABOUT ...

How do you think this movie might be different if it were made today? How have times changed, and how are they similar?

Song of the Sea

Beautiful Irish tale explores myths, sibling relationship.

 age 7+ ★★★★☆

A beautifully hand-drawn animation about Irish myths and legends with powerful messages about the importance of sibling relationships, accepting everything you feel (no matter how sad or scary), finding your voice, and doing everything to protect the people you love.

 Positive messages

 Positive role models

 Violence & scariness

Director: Tomm Moore

Cast: Brendan Gleeson, David Rawle, Fionnula Flanagan

Running time: 93 minutes

Release year: 2014

Genre: Animation

MPAA rating: PG

FAMILIES CAN TALK ABOUT ...

What is the movie saying about strong feelings? Are they something that should be repressed or embraced?

The Sound of Music

Outstanding family film features glorious music.

 age 6+   ★★★★★

This beloved, classic musical tells the story of Maria (Julie Andrews), an Austrian nun who's sent away to be the governess for seven uncooperative children. Maria wins them over, sharing her love of music and teaching them to sing — and helping to save them when the Nazis come.

 Positive messages

 Positive role models

Director: Robert Wise
Cast: Charmian Carr, Christopher Plummer, Julie Andrews
Running time: 174 minutes
Release year: 1965
Genre: Musical
MPAA rating: NR

FAMILIES CAN TALK ABOUT ...

If you were going to write the song "My Favorite Things," what would be on your list?

Spellbound

Families should see this m-a-r-v-e-l-o-u-s film.

 age 9+   ★★★★★

A documentary about the 1999 National Spelling Bee in Washington, D.C., and especially of eight regional winners. Every family should see this: It's about ambition, dedication, and courage as well as the strength of diversity and America's commitment to opportunity. Most of all, it's about family.

 Positive messages

Positive role models

Director: Jeffrey Blitz
Cast: Angela Arenivar, Neelima Marupudi, Ted Brigham
Running time: 96 minutes
Release year: 2003
Genre: Documentary
MPAA rating: G

FAMILIES CAN TALK ABOUT ...

What qualities do the kids in the movie share? What sacrifices do they and their families make?

Spider-Man

Fun movie, but may be too intense for younger kids.

 age 11+ ★★★★☆

On a school field trip, Peter Parker is bitten by a genetically engineered spider; the next morning he wakes up with some distinctly arachnid-like qualities. Toby Maguire is great as Peter, the supporting cast excels, and the script is excellent, with respect and affection for the source material.

 Positive messages

 Positive role models

 Violence & scariness

Director: Sam Raimi
Cast: Kirsten Dunst, Tobey Maguire, Willem Dafoe
Running time: 121 minutes
Release year: 2002
Genre: Action/Adventure
MPAA rating: PG-13

FAMILIES CAN TALK ABOUT ...

What does "with great power comes great responsibility" mean? Can you think of other superhero movies that tackle that theme?

Spirited Away

Magnificent movie with scary creatures and a strong heroine.

 age 9+ ★★★★★

Sullen 10-year-old Chihiro wanders into a world ruled by witches and monsters, where her parents gorge themselves on enchanted food and turn into pigs. She must overcome her whiny self to win them back. Hayao Miyazaki's magic adventure is an animated masterpiece but can be creepy for young viewers.

 Positive messages

 Positive role models

 Violence & scariness

Director: Hayao Miyazaki
Cast: Daveigh Chase, Jason Marsden, Suzanne Pleshette
Running time: 125 minutes
Release year: 2002
Genre: Animation
MPAA rating: PG

FAMILIES CAN TALK ABOUT ...

How does this movie compare to the average American animated film? What's different? What's similar?

Spy Kids

Just the right combination of fantasy and comedy.

 age 7+   ★★★★☆

Carmen and Juni, the children of the world's cleverest spies, must rescue their parents — and the entire world. This great family film has the right combination of fantasy, adventure, special effects, and sly comedy, and it's notable for featuring strong female and Latino characters.

 Positive messages

 Positive role models

 Violence & scariness

Director: Robert Rodriguez

Cast: Alexa Vega, Antonio Banderas, Daryl Sabara

Running time: 88 minutes

Release year: 2001

Genre: Action/Adventure

MPAA rating: PG

FAMILIES CAN TALK ABOUT ...

How does the violence in this movie compare to what you've seen in others? How does the fantasy element affect its impact?

Stand and Deliver

Intensely watchable movie based on a true story.

 age 13+   ★★★★☆

Based on the true story of an LA teacher who converted apathetic students into math stars. Full of Spanish, calculus, and inspiration, it brings depth and dignity to its exploration of high school life — rare in Hollywood. James Edward Olmos is near-perfect in an Oscar-nominated performance.

 Positive messages

 Positive role models

 Language

Director: Ramon Menendez

Cast: Andy Garcia, Edward James Olmos, Lou Diamond Phillips

Running time: 99 minutes

Release year: 1988

Genre: Drama

MPAA rating: PG

FAMILIES CAN TALK ABOUT ...

Can movies tell true stories in ways that other media, such as books or radio, can't? Who decides what's left out and what's emphasized?

Stand by Me

Edgy coming-of-age story not for young kids.

 age 14+ ★★★★

Four small-town, 12-year-old boys set out to find a dead body. Their unyielding camaraderie and irrepressible spirit see them through towering adversity. The film goes to considerable lengths to identify the issues and accurately portray the pressures that lead to teen disenchantment. Brilliant.

 Sexy stuff

 Language

 Drinking, drugs, & smoking

Director: Rob Reiner

Cast: Jerry O'Connell, River Phoenix, Wil Wheaton

Running time: 88 minutes

Release year: 1986

Genre: Drama

MPAA rating: R

FAMILIES CAN TALK ABOUT ...

Even though the movie is set many decades ago, do parts of it still feel relatable?

Star Wars: Episode IV: A New Hope

Sci-fi action classic perfect for sharing with kids.

 age 7+ ★★★★

Luke Skywalker, a lowly farm boy from the planet Tatooine, is swept into an intergalactic civil war after encountering two droids carrying secret plans for an engine of destruction known as the Death Star. A film whose story and characters have become sewn into the fabric of our popular culture.

 Positive messages

 Positive role models

 Violence & scariness

Director: George Lucas

Cast: Carrie Fisher, Harrison Ford, Mark Hamill

Running time: 120 minutes

Release year: 1977

Genre: Science Fiction

MPAA rating: PG

FAMILIES CAN TALK ABOUT ...

Movies have changed a lot since this film was released. Does it still seem exciting? Which parts (if any!) show their age?

Superman: The Movie

Super-nostalgic superhero adventure still soars.

 age 8+ ★★★★

Christopher Reeve proved an ideal Superman, with just the right level of steadfast simplicity. The film might be a bit slow for younger viewers, but the producers' emphasis on larger-than-life moviemaking (they won a Special Achievement Oscar for visual effects) spices up the well-known story.

 Positive messages

 Positive role models

 Violence & scariness

Director: Richard Donner
Cast: Christopher Reeve, Gene Hackman, Margot Kidder
Running time: 144 minutes
Release year: 1978
Genre: Action/Adventure
MPAA rating: PG

FAMILIES CAN TALK ABOUT ...

What makes a good superhero movie? Which ones are your favorites?

Swiss Family Robinson

Good intro to older movies for kids; watch for stereotypes.

 age 8+ ★★★★

When their ship washes ashore on a deserted island, the Robinson family must work together to survive. They build a tree house, raise farm animals, and explore for other sources of water. If you can get past the 1970s animation, this version tells the timeless tale of ingenuity and family bonding.

 Positive messages

 Positive role models

 Violence & scariness

Director: Ken Annakin
Cast: Dorothy McGuire, James MacArthur, John Mills
Running time: 126 minutes
Release year: 1960
Genre: Action/Adventure
MPAA rating: G

FAMILIES CAN TALK ABOUT ...

How has our culture changed since this movie was made? Why wouldn't the same characterizations be OK today?

Tangled

Fantastic princess adventure is fun, with great messages.

 age 5+

This reimagining of the classic Rapunzel tale is one Disney movie that's sure to entertain both boys and girls. The messages about girl power and seeing beyond appearances are positive and inspiring; kids will learn that we all have dreams and we should do everything we can to make them come true.

 Positive messages

 Positive role models

 Violence & scariness

Director: Byron Howard, Nathan Greno

Cast: Donna Murphy, Mandy Moore, Zachary Levi

Running time: 92 minutes

Release year: 2010

Genre: Animation

MPAA rating: PG

FAMILIES CAN TALK ABOUT ...

How is Rapunzel similar to and different from other Disney princesses? Is she the typical damsel in distress?

This Is Spinal Tap

Hilarious, ribald, drug-filled rock send-up.

 age 14+

Rob Reiner's classic "mockumentary" highlights the failure of a fictional band on its 1982 North America tour. The band is besieged by bad luck, and the members are so over the top it's impossible for anyone to take them seriously. Top-quality humor with classic scenes (these amps go to 11!).

 Sexy stuff

 Language

 Drinking, drugs, & smoking

Director: Rob Reiner

Cast: Christopher Guest, Harry Shearer, Michael McKean

Running time: 83 minutes

Release year: 1984

Genre: Comedy

MPAA rating: R

FAMILIES CAN TALK ABOUT ...

What's the difference between a documentary and a mockumentary? How can you tell which is which?

Titanic

Great movie, but not appropriate for all kids.

 age 13+

One of the highest-grossing films of all time is often considered a guilty pleasure, despite its 11 Oscars. But there's an irresistible love story starring two of the best actors of their generation (Leo DiCaprio and Kate Winslet); an evil villain; dazzling visual effects; and a soaring score.

 Violence & scariness

 Sexy stuff

 Language

Director: James Cameron

Cast: Billy Zane, Kate Winslet, Leonardo DiCaprio

Running time: 194 minutes

Release year: 1997

Genre: Romance

MPAA rating: PG-13

FAMILIES CAN TALK ABOUT ...

Has society's emphasis on class changed since the time period depicted here? Which other social considerations divide people today?

To Kill a Mockingbird

Masterpiece with crucial lessons about prejudice.

 age 12+

Set in a small Alabama town in the 1930s, the film explores prejudice and fear via the Finch family — 6-year-old Scout, her older brother Jem, and their widowed lawyer father Atticus Finch (Gregory Peck). A gentle goodness pervades despite the ugly truths portrayed. Based on Harper Lee's novel.

 Positive messages

 Positive role models

 Violence & scariness

 Language

Director: Robert Mulligan

Cast: Gregory Peck, Mary Badham, Robert Duvall

Running time: 131 minutes

Release year: 1962

Genre: Drama

MPAA rating: NR

FAMILIES CAN TALK ABOUT ...

How has the media's depiction of racism and people of varying races changed over the years? How has it not?

Toy Story

Pixar classic is one of the best kids' movies of all time.

 age 4+ ★★★★★

All is well with Andy's toys — especially Woody, his favorite — until Andy gets a special birthday present: toy spaceman Buzz Lightyear. Outstanding vocal performances and nonstop cleverness, with unpretentious imagination and energy.

 Positive messages

 Positive role models

 Violence & scariness

Director: John Lasseter

Cast: Don Rickles, Tim Allen, Tom Hanks

Running time: 81 minutes

Release year: 1995

Genre: Animation

MPAA rating: G

FAMILIES CAN TALK ABOUT ...

Do you really think that toys become "real" when humans leave the room? Why is imagination such an important part of playtime?

Up

Pixar's stunning adventure is an upper for everyone.

 age 6+ ★★★★★

After his beloved wife dies, Carl decides to live out her dream of visiting Paradise Falls. With hundreds of helium balloons, he mobilizes his house — and a young stowaway. Visually stunning, the movie truly soars in its telling of the sweet, funny, lasting relationship of its odd-couple heroes.

 Positive messages

Positive role models

Director: Pete Docter

Cast: Christopher Plummer, Ed Asner, Jordan Nagai

Running time: 98 minutes

Release year: 2009

Genre: Animation

MPAA rating: PG

FAMILIES CAN TALK ABOUT ...

What does the movie have to say about multigenerational friendships? What does Russell teach Carl and vice versa?

WALL-E

Brainy, charming, eco-friendly animated adventure.

 age 5+ ★★★★★

This deeply intellectual and profoundly moving adventure is charming — and nearly dialogue-free for the first half hour. A sanitation robot is the only citizen of a futuristic dystopia, until a spaceship drops off a lady robot. WALL-E falls in love — and may save mankind from unhealthy habits.

 Positive messages

 Positive role models

 Violence & scariness

---

Director: Andrew Stanton
Cast: Fred Willard, Jeff Garlin, Sigourney Weaver
Running time: 103 minutes
Release year: 2008
Genre: Animation
MPAA rating: G

FAMILIES CAN TALK ABOUT ...

What is the movie saying about the media's effect on people? Do you think the future humans in the movie were exaggerated to be funny, or could that really happen?

Wallace & Gromit in Three Amazing Adventures

Witty Claymation shorts with whole-family appeal.

 age 7+ ★★★★★

Tweens, teens, and adults will love the brilliant humor, action-adventure sequences, and complex, suspenseful plots of these three Claymation shorts, in which inventor and proper Englishman Wallace and his silent, wise dog Gromit brave a moon appliance, mechanical trousers, and a robotic dog.

Director: Nick Park
Cast: Anne Reid, Peter Sallis, Tristan Oliver
Running time: 85 minutes
Release year: 1990
Genre: Animation
MPAA rating: NR

FAMILIES CAN TALK ABOUT ...

What do you think would be some of the challenges in creating an animated movie using clay? How long would it take?

West Side Story

Musical masterpiece tackles race, with some violence.

 age 11+ ★★★★★

This classic American musical with strong social commentary updates Shakespeare's tragedy about star-crossed lovers Romeo and Juliet to 1950s New York City. With unforgettable music from Leonard Bernstein and Stephen Sondheim and Oscar-winning performances from George Chakiris and Rita Moreno.

 Positive messages

 Positive role models

 Drinking, drugs, & smoking

Director: Jerome Robbins
Cast: Natalie Wood, Richard Beymer, Rita Moreno
Running time: 152 minutes
Release year: 1961
Genre: Musical
MPAA rating: NR

FAMILIES CAN TALK ABOUT ...

What kinds of stereotypes are explored in this movie? Does the movie challenge or reinforce them?

Whale Rider

Excellent, gorgeous drama with uplifting messages.

 age 11+ ★★★★☆

Set in New Zealand, this is the story of 12-year-old Maori girl Paikaea, so named after her tribe's great leader over the objections of the chief when her twin brother and mother die in childbirth. The movie is not only genuinely lyrical but, even harder to manage, lyrically genuine.

 Sexy stuff

 Language

Director: Niki Caro
Cast: Keisha Castle-Hughes, Rawiri Paratene, Vicky Haughton
Running time: 105 minutes
Release year: 2003
Genre: Drama
MPAA rating: PG-13

FAMILIES CAN TALK ABOUT ...

Have you ever been told you couldn't do something because of your sex or age? How did you handle the issue?

When Harry Met Sally

Wit- and charm-filled romantic-comedy classic.

 age 14+ ★★★★☆

Over a period of 10 years, Harry and Sally bicker, become best friends, and eventually fall in love. Many have tried, but none has succeeded in capturing the charm, wit, and on-screen chemistry of this classic romantic comedy with a delightful script.

 Sexy stuff

 Language

Director: Rob Reiner
Cast: Billy Crystal, Carrie Fisher, Meg Ryan
Running time: 96 minutes
Release year: 1989
Genre: Comedy
MPAA rating: R

FAMILIES CAN TALK ABOUT ...

Is Harry correct in his theory that men and women can't be friends? How realistic is the outcome of Harry and Sally's relationship?

Willow

Magic-filled fantasy adventure with a few battle scenes.

 age 8+ ★★★★☆

Willow is a dwarf-like person whose children find a human baby who's the chosen one to bring down the reign of terror by the magical evil queen. Good triumphs over evil in this wonderful fantasy adventure with lots of intense battle scenes and conflict, often lightened with humor.

 Positive messages

 Positive role models

 Violence & scariness

Director: Ron Howard
Cast: Joanne Whalley, Val Kilmer, Warwick Davis
Running time: 126 minutes
Release year: 1988
Genre: Fantasy
MPAA rating: PG

FAMILIES CAN TALK ABOUT ...

How do the movie's jokes and silly pratfalls lessen the intensity of its violence and peril?

Willy Wonka and the Chocolate Factory

Pure, sweet imagination for both kids and adults.

 age 8+ ★★★★★

Reclusive candy mogul Willy Wonka leads impoverished Charlie and four other children on a tour of his factory. The other kids prove to be brats and suffer colorful fates. However, polite Charlie wins the factory, bringing his family out of poverty. A Roald Dahl classic.

 Positive messages

 Positive role models

 Violence & scariness

Director: Mel Stuart
Cast: Gene Wilder, Jack Albertson, Peter Ostrum
Running time: 98 minutes
Release year: 1971
Genre: Fantasy
MPAA rating: G

FAMILIES CAN TALK ABOUT ...

What would you do if you were one of the kids on the tour? When have you been rewarded for being honest?

The Wizard of Oz

Even decades later, one of the best family films ever made.

 age 6+ ★★★★★

This 1939 classic follows Dorothy (Judy Garland) from Kansas, where she's caught in a twister, to the land of Oz. She embarks down a yellow brick road, hoping to find the one person who can get her home. Memorable characters and a magic combination of drama, adventure, fantasy, and music.

 Positive messages

 Positive role models

Violence & scariness

Director: Victor Fleming
Cast: Bert Lahr, Jack Haley, Judy Garland, Ray Bolger
Running time: 101 minutes
Release year: 1939
Genre: Musical
MPAA rating: NR

FAMILIES CAN TALK ABOUT ...

How does the Scarecrow demonstrate his intelligence, the Tin Man his heart, and the Lion his courage? How does each one find what he needs within himself?

Yellow Submarine

Beatles classic with great animation, music.

 age 7+ ★★★★★

All is peace, love, and music in gentle Pepperland until the Blue Meanies take over. The Beatles come to the rescue, meeting all kinds of strange and interesting characters. A pleasure for the eye, ear, and heart, with spectacular animation, gorgeous music, witty wordplay, and a happy ending.

Director: George Dunning

Cast: John Lennon, Paul McCartney, Ringo Starr

Running time: 90 minutes

Release year: 1968

Genre: Animation

MPAA rating: G

FAMILIES CAN TALK ABOUT ...

Are there different ways to interpret this movie? Do you think there are hidden messages?

Young Frankenstein

Brooks' corniness yields plenty of belly laughs.

 age 10+ ★★★★★

Dr. Frederick Frankenstein gets word that he's inherited his famous ancestor's Transylvanian castle. There, he discovers a secret library containing his grandfather's notes on how to bring the dead to life — so he creates his own monster. Mel Brooks fans will rejoice at one of his funniest films.

 Sexy stuff

 Language

Director: Mel Brooks

Cast: Gene Wilder, Madeline Kahn, Marty Feldman, Peter Boyle

Running time: 105 minutes

Release year: 1974

Genre: Comedy

MPAA rating: PG

FAMILIES CAN TALK ABOUT ...

What makes this movie a parody? Is it patterned after old horror films? How does it differ?

MOVIES
BY TOPIC

Action, Adventure, and Thrills

The Adventures of Robin Hood  age 8+ ★★★★★
Errol Flynn stars in swashbuckling family delight.

Aladdin age 6+ ★★★★★
A magic carpet ride of a movie from Disney.

Big Hero 6 age 7+ ★★★★☆
Awesome origin story is action-packed, deals with grief.

Frankenstein age 10+ ★★★★★
Classic monster movie still electrifies.

Goldfinger age 13+ ★★★★☆
Thrilling action comedy may be the best Bond.

The Goonies age 10+ ★★★★☆
A classic '80s action-fantasy — tweens will love!

Homeward Bound: The Incredible Journey age 6+ ★★★★☆
Adventurous animal tale will have kids riveted.

How to Train Your Dragon age 7+ ★★★★☆
Thrilling 3-D adventure sends brains-over-brawn message.

Hugo age 8+ ★★★★★
Spectacular book adaptation is great for tweens and up.

Indiana Jones and the Raiders of the Lost Ark age 11+ ★★★★★
Indy's first adventure is a rip-roaring action masterpiece.

Jurassic Park age 12+ ★★★★☆
Terrifyingly realistic dinos run amok in sci-fi landmark.

The Lego Movie age 6+ ★★★★☆
Hilarious toy tale plugs product but is nonstop fun.

North by Northwest
Witty Hitchcock thriller piles on suspense and innuendo.

 age 11+ ★★★★

Pirates of the Caribbean: The Curse of the Black Pearl
Rip-roaring fun for kids who don't mind skeletons.

age 12+ ★★★★

Psycho
Horror masterpiece definitely isn't for young kids.

age 15+ ★★★★★

The Sixth Sense
Great, but sometimes scarier than R-rated horror.

age 14+ ★★★★

Spy Kids
Just the right combination of fantasy and comedy.

age 7+ ★★★★

Swiss Family Robinson
Good intro to older movies for kids; watch for stereotypes.

age 8+ ★★★★

Animal Tales

101 Dalmatians
Lovable cartoon classic with cute dogs and a mean villain.

age 5+ ★★★★★

Bambi
Disney's original circle-of-life story.

age 5+ ★★★★★

The Black Stallion
Breathtakingly beautiful and magical horse movie.

 age 8+ ★★★★★

Finding Nemo
Sweet father-son tale has some very scary moments.

age 5+ ★★★★★

Fly Away Home
Thrilling, touching adventure for animal lovers.

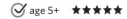 age 8+ ★★★★★

Lady and the Tramp
Classic Disney dogs paw their way into hearts of all ages.

✅ age 5+ ★★★★★

The Land Before Time
Baby dinosaur buddy flick that started the series.

✅ age 5+ ★★★★☆

The Lion King
Musical king-of-the-beasts blockbuster is powerful, scary.

✅ age 6+ ★★★★☆

The Many Adventures of Winnie the Pooh
Remains faithful to A. A. Milne's beloved classic stories.

✅ age 3+ ★★★★★

March of the Penguins
Stunning, loving documentary; some intense peril.

✅ age 6+ ★★★★★

National Velvet
Great family movie; even better for horse lovers.

✅ age 7+ ★★★★★

Old Yeller
Tearjerker is one of the best early Disney dramas.

✅ age 8+ ★★★★★

The Secret of NIMH
Fascinating, but very dark with some creepy imagery.

✅ age 8+ ★★★★☆

Classic Comedies

American Graffiti
Coming-of-age classic still a must-see for teens.

✅ age 13+ ★★★★★

Annie Hall
Classic comedy about relationships has mature themes.

✅ age 14+ ★★★★☆

Bringing Up Baby
Classic screwball comedy with loads of tame laughs.

✅ age 8+ ★★★★★

Dr. Strangelove: Or, How I Learned to Stop Worrying and Love the Bomb
Black-comedy Kubrick classic for smart teens+.
   age 14+ ★★★★★

Duck Soup
Classic comedy film with lots of mayhem, slapstick humor.
   age 7+ ★★★★★

The Graduate
Influential coming-of-age sex comedy.
   age 15+ ★★★★★

Modern Times
Families will cherish Chaplin's silent slapstick.
   age 6+ ★★★★★

Monty Python and the Holy Grail
Nonstop hilarity for families; some bawdy humor, profanity.
   age 13+ ★★★★★

The Muppet Movie
First Muppet movie is full of wonderful songs, plus guns.
   age 6+ ★★★★☆

The Parent Trap (1961)
Charming classic has some dated gender roles.
   age 6+ ★★★★☆

Some Like It Hot
One of the wildest romantic farces ever.
   age 11+ ★★★★★

This Is Spinal Tap
Hilarious, ribald, drug-filled rock send-up.
   age 14+ ★★★★☆

Yellow Submarine
Beatles classic with great animation, music.
   age 7+ ★★★★★

Young Frankenstein
Brooks' corniness yields plenty of belly laughs.
   age 10+ ★★★★★

Classic Dramas

Amadeus ✓ age 13+ ★★★★☆
Lavish, award-winning film with mature themes.

Citizen Kane ✓ age 12+ ★★★★★
Classic should be required for any movie lover.

Gandhi ✓ age 12+ ★★★★★
Brilliant biopic engages, educates, and inspires.

The Godfather ✓ age 16+ ★★★★★
The classic tale of a Mafia family, violence and all.

Gone with the Wind ✓ age 10+ ★★★★★
Still one of Hollywood's best sweeping epics.

Little Women (1949) ✓ age 9+ ★★★★☆
Adaptation of Alcott's story livened by superstar cast.

Network ✓ age 16+ ★★★★★
Biting '76 satire with a media-literacy lesson.

Rashomon ✓ age 15+ ★★★★★
Masterpiece about absolute truth. Best for teens.

Rebel Without a Cause ✓ age 13+ ★★★★★
1950s James Dean teen-rage landmark still resonates.

The Red Balloon ✓ age 7+ ★★★★★
Imaginative story told entirely through vivid visuals.

To Kill a Mockingbird ✓ age 12+ ★★★★★
Masterpiece with crucial lessons about prejudice.

Classic Musicals

Annie (1982)
Tale of cute orphan is great for the whole family.

 age 6+ ★★★★★

Chitty Chitty Bang Bang
A fantastical car story custom-made for kids.

age 6+ ★★★★☆

Fiddler on the Roof
Epic musical story of Jews facing religious persecution.

age 10+ ★★★★★

Grease
Musical phenomenon is great fun, but a bit racy.

age 12+ ★★★★☆

A Hard Day's Night
Beatles classic is Fab-ulous, but expect lots of smoking.

age 8+ ★★★★★

Mary Poppins
World's coolest nanny celebrates family and fun.

age 6+ ★★★★★

The Music Man
Glorious production with gorgeous music, dancing.

age 6+ ★★★★★

My Fair Lady
Witty, stylish musical classic will entertain all ages.

age 6+ ★★★★★

Oliver!
Glorious musical based on Dickens' *Oliver Twist*.

age 8+ ★★★★☆

Singin' in the Rain
Often considered the finest musical of all time.

age 6+ ★★★★★

The Sound of Music
Outstanding family film features glorious music.

age 6+ ★★★★★

West Side Story ✅ age 11+ ★★★★★
Musical masterpiece tackles race, with some violence.

The Wizard of Oz ✅ age 6+ ★★★★★
Even decades later, one of the best family films ever made.

Coming-of-Age Stories

Almost Famous ✅ age 16+ ★★★★★
Great, but lots of sex, drugs, and rock 'n' roll.

Billy Elliot ✅ age 13+ ★★★★☆
Terrific story of young ballet dancer has strong language.

Boyhood ✅ age 15+ ★★★★★
Unique, affecting, mature drama about life and growing up.

Dead Poets Society ✅ age 13+ ★★★★☆
Inspiring, intense story of a teacher and his students.

Drumline ✅ age 12+ ★★★★☆
Outstanding cast, great message, strong language.

Good Will Hunting ✅ age 15+ ★★★★★
Moving story of brilliant, troubled youth for older teens.

Inside Out ✅ age 6+ ★★★★★
Beautiful, original story about handling big feelings.

Lucas ✅ age 13+ ★★★★★
A realistic look at a teen's coming-of-age.

Millions ✅ age 10+ ★★★★★
A beautiful, rare family film that everyone can enjoy.

October Sky ✓ age 10+ ★★★★★
Inspiring tale for older tweens and up.

Real Women Have Curves ✓ age 14+ ★★★★★
Ugly Betty star captivates in teen drama.

Fairy Tales

Beauty and the Beast ✓ age 5+ ★★★★★
The ultimate makeover story has strong, positive messages.

Cinderella ✓ age 5+ ★★★★★
Sweet fairy-tale classic for little princes and princesses.

The Little Mermaid ✓ age 5+ ★★★★★
Superb, entertaining animated musical has some scary stuff.

Pinocchio ✓ age 6+ ★★★★★
Disney masterpiece is darker than you may remember.

The Princess Bride ✓ age 8+ ★★★★★
Witty, winsome fairy tale for the whole family.

Shrek ✓ age 6+ ★★★★★
Gross-out laughs meet a marvelous fairy-tale mix.

Snow White and the Seven Dwarfs ✓ age 5+ ★★★★☆
Animated classic is enchanting but also scary.

Tangled ✓ age 5+ ★★★★★
Fantastic princess adventure is fun, with great messages.

Foreign Films

Children of Heaven
Excellent subtitled Iranian coming-of-age story.
⊘ age 10+ ★★★★★

Cinema Paradiso
Charming Italian film about friendship, movies.
⊘ age 13+ ★★★★☆

Crouching Tiger, Hidden Dragon
Magical, award-winning martial-arts fairy tale.
⊘ age 12+ ★★★★★

Howl's Moving Castle
Charming Miyazaki fairy tale with surreal villains.
⊘ age 8+ ★★★★☆

My Neighbor Totoro
Beautifully animated fantasy about friendship fit for all.
⊘ age 5+ ★★★★★

Song of the Sea
Beautiful Irish tale explores myths, sibling relationship.
⊘ age 7+ ★★★★☆

Spirited Away
Magnificent movie with scary creatures and a strong heroine.
⊘ age 9+ ★★★★★

Friendship Tales

The Adventures of Milo and Otis
Lovable pet tale about friendship despite differences.
⊘ age 5+ ★★★★★

Charlotte's Web (2006)
Enchanting take on a beloved children's classic.
⊘ age 5+ ★★★★★

The Iron Giant
Touching robot-kid friendship tale with great messages.
⊘ age 6+ ★★★★☆

Monsters, Inc.
Cute, kid-friendly monster movie; may scare sensitive kids.
 age 5+ ★★★★☆

The Shawshank Redemption
Gritty but comforting story of friendship.
age 15+ ★★★★☆

The Sisterhood of the Traveling Pants
Sensitive portrayal of four girls' friendships.
age 12+ ★★★★☆

Stand by Me
Edgy coming-of-age story not for young kids.
age 14+ ★★★★☆

Toy Story
Pixar classic is one of the best kids' movies of all time.
 age 4+ ★★★★★

Up
Pixar's stunning adventure is an upper for everyone.
 age 6+ ★★★★★

High School Stories

The Breakfast Club
Socially relevant '80s teen flick.
age 15+ ★★★★☆

Clueless
Charming, funny take on Jane Austen's *Emma*.
age 14+ ★★★★☆

Ferris Bueller's Day Off
Despite language, iffy behavior, this is a comedy classic.
age 12+ ★★★★★

High School Musical
A modern-day *Grease* for tweens.
age 8+ ★★★★☆

Juno
Brilliant teen-pregnancy comedy, but iffy for kids.
age 14+ ★★★★★

Mean Girls 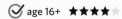 age 14+ ★★★★
Mature but often-hilarious teen comedy.

Sixteen Candles age 16+ ★★★★
Racy, drunken, hilarious '80s high school comedy.

Holiday Favorites

A Charlie Brown Christmas age 3+ ★★★★★
The Peanuts gang in a classic Christmas special.

A Christmas Story age 8+ ★★★★★
Wonderful antidote to cutesy holiday tales; some swearing.

Dr. Seuss' How the Grinch Stole Christmas age 4+ ★★★★★
Heartwarming TV special true to Seuss' classic.

Elf age 7+ ★★★★
Peppy holiday favorite for both kids and parents.

Home Alone age 7+ ★★★★
Slapstick family holiday comedy brings the pain.

It's a Wonderful Life age 9+ ★★★★★
This classic delivers warmth all year long.

Miracle on 34th Street age 6+ ★★★★
Classic holiday movie for the whole family.

The Nightmare Before Christmas age 7+ ★★★★★
Tim Burton magic with just a touch of scariness.

Laugh Out Louds

Babe ✓ age 6+ ★★★★★
Heartwarming farm story is touching and a bit scary.

Barbershop ✓ age 13+ ★★★★☆
Charming urban comedy for teens.

Big ✓ age 13+ ★★★★☆
Wonderful story with some very mature material.

Chicken Run ✓ age 7+ ★★★★☆
Charming animated escape tale has some peril, scares.

Ghostbusters ✓ age 11+ ★★★★☆
Paranormal '80s classic has some scares, innuendo.

Groundhog Day ✓ age 11+ ★★★★★
'90s comedy offers witty, sarcastic take on redemption.

Mrs. Doubtfire ✓ age 12+ ★★★★☆
You'll laugh, you'll cry. Best divorce movie.

Napoleon Dynamite ✓ age 11+ ★★★★☆
One-of-a-kind high school comedy for the family.

Pee-Wee's Big Adventure ✓ age 7+ ★★★★☆
Just as charming and curious as it was in 1985.

School of Rock ✓ age 11+ ★★★★☆
Standout Jack Black in nerds-become-cool comedy.

Wallace & Gromit in Three Amazing Adventures ✓ age 7+ ★★★★★
Witty Claymation shorts with whole-family appeal.

Love Stories

Casablanca  age 10+ ★★★★★
Brief violence and lots of tension in top-notch classic.

Moulin Rouge  age 15+ ★★★★☆
Dazzling musical romance for teens.

Pride & Prejudice  age 11+ ★★★★☆
Gorgeous Jane Austen adaptation has timeless appeal.

Roman Holiday  age 9+ ★★★★★
Delightful classic is perfect for family movie night.

Say Anything  age 15+ ★★★★★
A gem of a coming-of-age story.

Sense and Sensibility 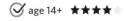 age 11+ ★★★★★
A lush and witty adaptation of Jane Austen's novel.

Titanic age 13+ ★★★★☆
Great movie, but not appropriate for all kids.

When Harry Met Sally age 14+ ★★★★☆
Wit- and charm-filled romantic-comedy classic.

Sci-Fi and Fantasy

Alice in Wonderland age 4+ ★★★★☆
Surreal animated Disney classic with mild peril.

Back to the Future age 10+ ★★★★★
'80s time-travel favorite has laughs, romance, action.

Blade Runner
A dark, philosophical sci-fi drama for older teens.
✓ age 16+ ★★★★☆

Close Encounters of the Third Kind
Suspenseful, thoughtful alien-encounter classic.
✓ age 8+ ★★★★★

The Dark Crystal
A fantastic but more intense Muppet adventure.
✓ age 7+ ★★★★☆

Edward Scissorhands
Dark yet sweet underdog tale for older kids.
✓ age 13+ ★★★★☆

E.T.: The Extra-Terrestrial
Spielberg's family classic is still one of the best.
✓ age 7+ ★★★★★

Fantasia
Breathtaking animation feat — with some creepy visuals.
✓ age 6+ ★★★★★

Harry Potter and the Sorcerer's Stone
First Potter movie is a magical ride but also intense.
✓ age 7+ ★★★★★

The Indian in the Cupboard
Classic, heartwarming fantasy will rivet kids.
✓ age 7+ ★★★★★

James and the Giant Peach
Fabulous adaptation of Roald Dahl's classic book.
✓ age 7+ ★★★★☆

The Lord of the Rings: The Fellowship of the Ring
Fabulous, but also violent and scary.
✓ age 12+ ★★★★★

Matilda
Offbeat fantasy gem, but too dark for young kids.
✓ age 8+ ★★★★★

The NeverEnding Story
Boy bibliophile becomes part of fantasy tale.
✓ age 8+ ★★★★☆

Star Wars: Episode IV: A New Hope
Sci-fi action classic perfect for sharing with kids.
✓ age 7+ ★★★★☆

WALL-E
Brainy, charming, eco-friendly animated adventure.

age 5+ ★★★★★

Willow
Magic-filled fantasy adventure with a few battle scenes.

age 8+ ★★★★☆

Willy Wonka and the Chocolate Factory
Pure, sweet imagination for both kids and adults.

age 8+ ★★★★★

Sports Movies

Bend It Like Beckham
Superb tale of a girl's struggle for her dreams.

age 13+ ★★★★☆

Hoop Dreams
Stunning documentary, great for older kids.

age 13+ ★★★★★

Hoosiers
Stirring tale of heroic sportsmanship will inspire families.

age 9+ ★★★★★

The Karate Kid
'80s classic is still fun for families with older tweens.

age 11+ ★★★★☆

A League of Their Own
Terrific tweens-and-up story of women's baseball.

age 10+ ★★★★☆

Remember the Titans
Inspiring football drama brings history to life.

age 10+ ★★★★☆

Rudy
Inspiring sports film about a real-life underdog.

age 11+ ★★★★★

The Sandlot
Field of Dreams for tweens.

age 8+ ★★★★☆

Strong Girls

Akeelah and the Bee
Inspiring drama about a champion speller; OK for tweens.
age 8+ ★★★★

Anne of Green Gables
Faithful, sensitive take on classic novel is great for kids.
age 7+ ★★★★★

Frozen
Wintry Disney musical is fabulous celebration of sisterhood.
age 5+ ★★★★★

The Hunger Games
Intense adaptation is violent, thought-provoking for teens.
age 14+ ★★★★★

A Little Princess
Wonderful adaptation of classic book; some scary moments.
age 7+ ★★★★

Mulan
Disneyfied but dignified tale of Chinese warrior.
age 5+ ★★★★

The Princess Diaries
Sweet tale about growing up is terrific fun for families.
age 8+ ★★★★★

Whale Rider
Excellent, gorgeous drama with uplifting messages.
age 11+ ★★★★

Superheroes

The Avengers
Heroes work together in explosive comic-book adventure.
age 13+ ★★★★

The Dark Knight
Excellent sequel much darker, more violent than the first.
age 15+ ★★★★★

The Incredibles ✓ age 7+ ★★★★★
Top-notch, action-packed fun for the entire family.

Iron Man ✓ age 13+ ★★★★☆
Great action, lots of style, some iffy stuff.

Spider-Man ✓ age 11+ ★★★★☆
Fun movie, but may be too intense for younger kids.

Superman: The Movie ✓ age 8+ ★★★★☆
Super-nostalgic superhero adventure still soars.

Thoughtful Dramas

About a Boy ✓ age 14+ ★★★★☆
Grant grows a heart in Hornby-book pic; teens+.

The Color Purple ✓ age 14+ ★★★★★
Powerful tale of survival with wrenching scenes of abuse.

Do the Right Thing ✓ age 16+ ★★★★☆
Spike Lee's masterwork of racial unrest; discuss with kids.

Forrest Gump ✓ age 13+ ★★★★★
Moving and wonderful, but parent preview a good idea.

The Namesake ✓ age 14+ ★★★★★
Fabulous immigrant-family saga to see with teens.

Slumdog Millionaire ✓ age 16+ ★★★★★
Epic romance-drama is brilliant but too mature for kids.

True Stories

The King's Speech ✅ age 14+ ★★★★★
Superb drama about overcoming fears is fine for teens.

Lincoln ✅ age 13+ ★★★★★
Outstanding story about revered leader's political genius.

Mad Hot Ballroom ✅ age 8+ ★★★★★
Enchanting dance documentary hits all the right beats.

The Pianist ✅ age 16+ ★★★★★
True story of a Jewish pianist; OK for older kids.

Schindler's List ✅ age 15+ ★★★★★
Accurate, heartbreaking masterpiece about the Holocaust.

Selena ✅ age 10+ ★★★★
Touching and ultimately tragic tale of young Tejano star.

Selma ✅ age 13+ ★★★★★
Outstanding drama about MLK's fight for equal rights.

Spellbound ✅ age 9+ ★★★★★
Families should see this m-a-r-v-e-l-o-u-s film.

Stand and Deliver ✅ age 13+ ★★★★
Intensely watchable movie based on a true story.

MOVIES
BY AGE

Little Kids: Age 3-6

A Charlie Brown Christmas   ⊘ age 3+   ★★★★★
The Peanuts gang in a classic Christmas special.

The Many Adventures of Winnie the Pooh   ⊘ age 3+   ★★★★★
Remains faithful to A. A. Milne's beloved classic stories.

Alice in Wonderland   ⊘ age 4+   ★★★★☆
Surreal animated Disney classic with mild peril.

Dr. Seuss' How the Grinch Stole Christmas   ⊘ age 4+   ★★★★★
Heartwarming TV special true to Seuss' classic.

Toy Story   ⊘ age 4+   ★★★★★
Pixar classic is one of the best kids' movies of all time.

101 Dalmatians   ⊘ age 5+   ★★★★★
Lovable cartoon classic with cute dogs and a mean villain.

The Adventures of Milo and Otis   ⊘ age 5+   ★★★★★
Lovable pet tale about friendship despite differences.

Bambi   ⊘ age 5+   ★★★★★
Disney's original circle-of-life story.

Beauty and the Beast   ⊘ age 5+   ★★★★★
The ultimate makeover story has strong, positive messages.

Charlotte's Web (2006)   ⊘ age 5+   ★★★★★
Enchanting take on a beloved children's classic.

Cinderella   ⊘ age 5+   ★★★★★
Sweet fairy-tale classic for little princes and princesses.

Many animated films are based on books. Hone reading skills with a familiar, favorite story.

Finding Nemo ☑ age 5+ ★★★★★
Sweet father-son tale has some very scary moments.

Frozen ☑ age 5+ ★★★★★
Wintry Disney musical is fabulous celebration of sisterhood.

> **Ask kids if a character feels less real because it's a cartoon. Can they care about Nemo or Bambi?**

Lady and the Tramp ☑ age 5+ ★★★★★
Classic Disney dogs paw their way into hearts of all ages.

The Land Before Time ☑ age 5+ ★★★★
Baby dinosaur buddy flick that started the series.

The Little Mermaid ☑ age 5+ ★★★★★
Superb, entertaining animated musical has some scary stuff.

Monsters, Inc. ☑ age 5+ ★★★★
Cute, kid-friendly monster movie; may scare sensitive kids.

Mulan ☑ age 5+ ★★★★
Disneyfied but dignified tale of Chinese warrior.

My Neighbor Totoro ☑ age 5+ ★★★★★
Beautifully animated fantasy about friendship fit for all.

Snow White and the Seven Dwarfs ☑ age 5+ ★★★★
Animated classic is enchanting but also scary.

Tangled ☑ age 5+ ★★★★★
Fantastic princess adventure is fun, with great messages.

WALL-E ☑ age 5+ ★★★★★
Brainy, charming, eco-friendly animated adventure.

Aladdin ☑ age 6+ ★★★★
A magic carpet ride of a movie from Disney.

Ask kids if Babe or Milo would make a good pet. Why might a dog be better than a penguin ... or worse?

Annie (1982)   age 6+   ★★★★★
Tale of cute orphan is great for the whole family.

Babe   age 6+   ★★★★☆
Heartwarming farm story is touching and a bit scary.

Chitty Chitty Bang Bang   age 6+   ★★★★☆
A fantastical car story custom-made for kids.

Fantasia   age 6+   ★★★★★
Breathtaking animation feat — with some creepy visuals.

Homeward Bound: The Incredible Journey   age 6+   ★★★★☆
Adventurous animal tale will have kids riveted.

Inside Out   age 6+   ★★★★★
Beautiful, original story about handling big feelings.

The Iron Giant   age 6+   ★★★★☆
Touching robot-kid friendship tale with great messages.

The Lego Movie   age 6+   ★★★★☆
Hilarious toy tale plugs product but is nonstop fun.

The Lion King   age 6+   ★★★★☆
Musical king-of-the-beasts blockbuster is powerful, scary.

March of the Penguins   age 6+   ★★★★★
Stunning, loving documentary; some intense peril.

Mary Poppins   age 6+   ★★★★★
World's coolest nanny celebrates family and fun.

Miracle on 34th Street   age 6+   ★★★★☆
Classic holiday movie for the whole family.

Modern Times ✅ age 6+ ★★★★★
Families will cherish Chaplin's silent slapstick.

The Muppet Movie ✅ age 6+ ★★★★
First Muppet movie is full of wonderful songs, plus guns.

The Music Man ✅ age 6+ ★★★★★
Glorious production with gorgeous music, dancing.

My Fair Lady ✅ age 6+ ★★★★★
Witty, stylish musical classic will entertain all ages.

The Parent Trap (1961) ✅ age 6+ ★★★★
Charming classic has some dated gender roles.

Pinocchio ✅ age 6+ ★★★★★
Disney masterpiece is darker than you may remember.

Shrek ✅ age 6+ ★★★★★
Gross-out laughs meet a marvelous fairy-tale mix.

Singin' in the Rain ✅ age 6+ ★★★★★
Often considered the finest musical of all time.

The Sound of Music ✅ age 6+ ★★★★★
Outstanding family film features glorious music.

Up ✅ age 6+ ★★★★★
Pixar's stunning adventure is an upper for everyone.

The Wizard of Oz ✅ age 6+ ★★★★★
Even decades later, one of the best family films ever made.

Plan a soundtrack sing-along with some classic favorites ("The hills are alive ... !").

Big Kids & Tweens: Age 7-12

Anne of Green Gables   ✅ age 7+   ★★★★★
Faithful, sensitive take on classic novel is great for kids.

Big Hero 6   ✅ age 7+   ★★★★
Awesome origin story is action-packed, deals with grief.

Chicken Run   ✅ age 7+   ★★★★
Charming animated escape tale has some peril, scares.

The Dark Crystal   ✅ age 7+   ★★★★
A fantastic but more intense Muppet adventure.

Duck Soup   ✅ age 7+   ★★★★★
Classic comedy film with lots of mayhem, slapstick humor.

E.T.: The Extra-Terrestrial   ✅ age 7+   ★★★★★
Spielberg's family classic is still one of the best.

Elf   ✅ age 7+   ★★★★
Peppy holiday favorite for both kids and parents.

Harry Potter and the Sorcerer's Stone   ✅ age 7+   ★★★★★
First Potter movie is a magical ride but also intense.

> Dress in costume for *A Princess Bride*, or learn a few magic tricks before *Harry Potter*.

Home Alone   ✅ age 7+   ★★★★
Slapstick family holiday comedy brings the pain.

How to Train Your Dragon   ✅ age 7+   ★★★★
Thrilling 3-D adventure sends brains-over-brawn message.

The Incredibles   ✅ age 7+   ★★★★★
Top-notch, action-packed fun for the entire family.

The Indian in the Cupboard
✅ age 7+   ★★★★★
Classic, heartwarming fantasy will rivet kids.

James and the Giant Peach
✅ age 7+   ★★★★
Fabulous adaptation of Roald Dahl's classic book.

A Little Princess
✅ age 7+   ★★★★
Wonderful adaptation of classic book; some scary moments.

National Velvet
✅ age 7+   ★★★★★
Great family movie; even better for horse lovers.

Ask your kids why these movies have lasting value. How are they still relevant, and how are they not?

The Nightmare Before Christmas
✅ age 7+   ★★★★★
Tim Burton magic with just a touch of scariness.

Pee-Wee's Big Adventure
✅ age 7+   ★★★★
Just as charming and curious as it was in 1985.

The Red Balloon
✅ age 7+   ★★★★★
Imaginative story told entirely through vivid visuals.

Song of the Sea
✅ age 7+   ★★★★
Beautiful Irish tale explores myths, sibling relationship.

Spy Kids
✅ age 7+   ★★★★
Just the right combination of fantasy and comedy.

Star Wars: Episode IV: A New Hope
✅ age 7+   ★★★★
Sci-fi action classic perfect for sharing with kids.

Wallace & Gromit in Three Amazing Adventures
✅ age 7+   ★★★★★
Witty Claymation shorts with whole-family appeal.

Yellow Submarine
✅ age 7+   ★★★★★
Beatles classic with great animation, music.

The Adventures of Robin Hood ☑ age 8+ ★★★★★
Errol Flynn stars in swashbuckling family delight.

Akeelah and the Bee ☑ age 8+ ★★★★
Inspiring drama about a champion speller; OK for tweens.

The Black Stallion ☑ age 8+ ★★★★★
Breathtakingly beautiful and magical horse movie.

Bringing Up Baby ☑ age 8+ ★★★★★
Classic screwball comedy with loads of tame laughs.

A Christmas Story ☑ age 8+ ★★★★★
Wonderful antidote to cutesy holiday tales; some swearing.

Close Encounters of the Third Kind ☑ age 8+ ★★★★★
Suspenseful, thoughtful alien-encounter classic.

Fly Away Home ☑ age 8+ ★★★★★
Thrilling, touching adventure for animal lovers.

A Hard Day's Night ☑ age 8+ ★★★★★
Beatles classic is Fab-ulous, but expect lots of smoking.

High School Musical ☑ age 8+ ★★★★
A modern-day *Grease* for tweens.

Howl's Moving Castle ☑ age 8+ ★★★★
Charming Miyazaki fairy tale with surreal villains.

Hugo ☑ age 8+ ★★★★★
Spectacular book adaptation is great for tweens and up.

Mad Hot Ballroom ☑ age 8+ ★★★★★
Enchanting dance documentary hits all the right beats.

Matilda
Offbeat fantasy gem, but too dark for young kids.
✓ age 8+ ★★★★★

The NeverEnding Story
Boy bibliophile becomes part of fantasy tale.
✓ age 8+ ★★★★☆

Old Yeller
Tearjerker is one of the best early Disney dramas.
✓ age 8+ ★★★★★

Oliver!
Glorious musical based on Dickens' *Oliver Twist*.
✓ age 8+ ★★★★☆

The Princess Bride
Witty, winsome fairy tale for the whole family.
✓ age 8+ ★★★★★

The Princess Diaries
Sweet tale about growing up is terrific fun for families.
✓ age 8+ ★★★★★

The Sandlot
Field of Dreams for tweens.
✓ age 8+ ★★★★☆

The Secret of NIMH
Fascinating, but very dark with some creepy imagery.
✓ age 8+ ★★★★☆

Practice your poker face during difficult scenes — kids get more scared when you look anxious.

Superman: The Movie
Super-nostalgic superhero adventure still soars.
✓ age 8+ ★★★★☆

Swiss Family Robinson
Good intro to older movies for kids; watch for stereotypes.
✓ age 8+ ★★★★☆

Willow
Magic-filled fantasy adventure with a few battle scenes.
✓ age 8+ ★★★★☆

Willy Wonka and the Chocolate Factory
Pure, sweet imagination for both kids and adults.
✓ age 8+ ★★★★★

Hoosiers ☑ age 9+ ★★★★★
Stirring tale of heroic sportsmanship will inspire families.

It's a Wonderful Life ☑ age 9+ ★★★★★
This classic delivers warmth all year long.

Little Women (1949) ☑ age 9+ ★★★★☆
Adaptation of Alcott's story livened by superstar cast.

Roman Holiday ☑ age 9+ ★★★★★
Delightful classic is perfect for family movie night.

Spellbound ☑ age 9+ ★★★★★
Families should see this m-a-r-v-e-l-o-u-s film.

Spirited Away ☑ age 9+ ★★★★★
Magnificent movie with scary creatures and a strong heroine.

Back to the Future ☑ age 10+ ★★★★★
'80s time-travel favorite has laughs, romance, action.

Casablanca ☑ age 10+ ★★★★★
Brief violence and lots of tension in top-notch classic.

Children of Heaven ☑ age 10+ ★★★★★
Excellent subtitled Iranian coming-of-age story.

Fiddler on the Roof ☑ age 10+ ★★★★★
Epic musical story of Jews facing religious persecution.

Frankenstein ☑ age 10+ ★★★★★
Classic monster movie still electrifies.

Gone with the Wind ☑ age 10+ ★★★★★
Still one of Hollywood's best sweeping epics.

Learn Napoleon Dynamite's sweet dance moves and hold a talent show.

The Goonies
A classic '80s action-fantasy — tweens will love!

✓ age 10+ ★★★★☆

A League of Their Own
Terrific tweens-and-up story of women's baseball.

✓ age 10+ ★★★★☆

Millions
A beautiful, rare family film that everyone can enjoy.

✓ age 10+ ★★★★★

October Sky
Inspiring tale for older tweens and up.

✓ age 10+ ★★★★★

What does it mean to "come of age"? Do you feel like you're coming of age?

Remember the Titans
Inspiring football drama brings history to life.

✓ age 10+ ★★★★☆

Selena
Touching and ultimately tragic tale of young Tejano star.

✓ age 10+ ★★★★☆

Young Frankenstein
Brooks' corniness yields plenty of belly laughs.

✓ age 10+ ★★★★★

Ghostbusters
Paranormal '80s classic has some scares, innuendo.

✓ age 11+ ★★★★☆

Groundhog Day
'90s comedy offers witty, sarcastic take on redemption.

✓ age 11+ ★★★★★

Indiana Jones and the Raiders of the Lost Ark
Indy's first adventure is a rip-roaring action masterpiece.

✓ age 11+ ★★★★★

The Karate Kid
'80s classic is still fun for families with older tweens.

✓ age 11+ ★★★★☆

Napoleon Dynamite
One-of-a-kind high school comedy for the family.

✓ age 11+ ★★★★☆

North by Northwest
Witty Hitchcock thriller piles on suspense and innuendo.

age 11+ ★★★★☆

Pride & Prejudice
Gorgeous Jane Austen adaptation has timeless appeal.

age 11+ ★★★★☆

Rudy
Inspiring sports film about a real-life underdog.

age 11+ ★★★★★

School of Rock
Standout Jack Black in nerds-become-cool comedy.

age 11+ ★★★★☆

Sense and Sensibility
A lush and witty adaptation of Jane Austen's novel.

age 11+ ★★★★★

Some Like It Hot
One of the wildest romantic farces ever.

age 11+ ★★★★★

Spider-Man
Fun movie, but may be too intense for younger kids.

age 11+ ★★★★☆

West Side Story
Musical masterpiece tackles race, with some violence.

age 11+ ★★★★★

Whale Rider
Excellent, gorgeous drama with uplifting messages.

age 11+ ★★★★☆

Apollo 13
Thrilling, heartwarming, scary, and superb.

age 12+ ★★★★★

Citizen Kane
Classic should be required for any movie lover.

age 12+ ★★★★★

Crouching Tiger, Hidden Dragon
Magical, award-winning martial-arts fairy tale.

age 12+ ★★★★★

Drumline
Outstanding cast, great message, strong language.

age 12+ ★★★★☆

Ferris Bueller's Day Off ✓ age 12+ ★★★★★
Despite language, iffy behavior, this is a comedy classic.

Gandhi ✓ age 12+ ★★★★★
Brilliant biopic engages, educates, and inspires.

> Discuss the historical context of *Gandhi*. What was his goal?
> What do you think about his methods?

Grease ✓ age 12+ ★★★★
Musical phenomenon is great fun, but a bit racy.

Jurassic Park ✓ age 12+ ★★★★
Terrifyingly realistic dinos run amok in sci-fi landmark.

The Lord of the Rings: The Fellowship of the Ring ✓ age 12+ ★★★★★
Fabulous, but also violent and scary.

Mrs. Doubtfire ✓ age 12+ ★★★★
You'll laugh, you'll cry. Best divorce movie.

Pirates of the Caribbean: The Curse of the Black Pearl ✓ age 12+ ★★★★
Rip-roaring fun for kids who don't mind skeletons.

The Sisterhood of the Traveling Pants ✓ age 12+ ★★★★
Sensitive portrayal of four girls' friendships.

To Kill a Mockingbird ✓ age 12+ ★★★★★
Masterpiece with crucial lessons about prejudice.

Teens: Age 13+

Amadeus
Lavish, award-winning film with mature themes.
✓ age 13+ ★★★★☆

American Graffiti
Coming-of-age classic still a must-see for teens.
✓ age 13+ ★★★★★

The Avengers
Heroes work together in explosive comic-book adventure.
✓ age 13+ ★★★★☆

> **Even a movie based on a comic book can be extremely violent. Is there "good" and "bad" violence?**

Barbershop
Charming urban comedy for teens.
✓ age 13+ ★★★★☆

Bend It Like Beckham
Superb tale of a girl's struggle for her dreams.
✓ age 13+ ★★★★☆

Big
Wonderful story with some very mature material.
✓ age 13+ ★★★★☆

Billy Elliot
Terrific story of young ballet dancer has strong language.
✓ age 13+ ★★★★☆

Cinema Paradiso
Charming Italian film about friendship, movies.
✓ age 13+ ★★★★☆

Dead Poets Society
Inspiring, intense story of a teacher and his students.
✓ age 13+ ★★★★☆

Edward Scissorhands
Dark yet sweet underdog tale for older kids.
✓ age 13+ ★★★★☆

Forrest Gump
Moving and wonderful, but parent preview a good idea.
✓ age 13+ ★★★★★

Goldfinger
Thrilling action comedy may be the best Bond.
✅ age 13+ ★★★★

Hoop Dreams
Stunning documentary, great for older kids.
✅ age 13+ ★★★★★

Iron Man
Great action, lots of style, some iffy stuff.
✅ age 13+ ★★★★

Lincoln
Outstanding drama about revered leader's political genius.
✅ age 13+ ★★★★★

Lucas
A realistic look at a teen's coming-of-age.
✅ age 13+ ★★★★★

Monty Python and the Holy Grail
Nonstop hilarity for families; some bawdy humor, profanity.
✅ age 13+ ★★★★★

Rebel Without a Cause
1950s James Dean teen-rage landmark still resonates.
✅ age 13+ ★★★★★

Selma
Outstanding drama about MLK's fight for equal rights.
✅ age 13+ ★★★★★

Stand and Deliver
Intensely watchable movie based on a true story.
✅ age 13+ ★★★★

> **Are these teens' stories simple or complex? Can you relate to their issues with school, friends, and parents?**

Titanic
Great movie, but not appropriate for all kids.
✅ age 13+ ★★★★

About a Boy
Grant grows a heart in Hornby-book pic; teens+.
✅ age 14+ ★★★★

Annie Hall
Classic comedy about relationships has mature themes.
✅ age 14+ ★★★★

Clueless ☑ age 14+ ★★★★
Charming, funny take on Jane Austen's *Emma*.

The Color Purple ☑ age 14+ ★★★★★
Powerful tale of survival with wrenching scenes of abuse.

> **Schedule a time to watch an intense film. Ban multitasking, and then discuss difficult scenes.**

Dr. Strangelove: Or, How I Learned to Stop Worrying and Love the Bomb ☑ age 14+ ★★★★★
Black-comedy Kubrick classic for smart teens+.

The Hunger Games ☑ age 14+ ★★★★★
Intense adaptation is violent, thought-provoking for teens.

Juno ☑ age 14+ ★★★★★
Brilliant teen-pregnancy comedy, but iffy for kids.

The King's Speech ☑ age 14+ ★★★★★
Superb drama about overcoming fears is fine for teens.

Mean Girls ☑ age 14+ ★★★★
Mature but often-hilarious teen comedy.

The Namesake ☑ age 14+ ★★★★★
Fabulous immigrant-family saga to see with teens.

Real Women Have Curves ☑ age 14+ ★★★★★
Ugly Betty star captivates in teen drama.

> **Ask teens for their own examples of hardship or prejudice that help them relate to these movies.**

The Sixth Sense ☑ age 14+ ★★★★
Great, but sometimes scarier than R-rated horror.

Stand by Me
age 14+ ★★★★☆
Edgy coming-of-age story not for young kids.

This Is Spinal Tap
age 14+ ★★★★☆
Hilarious, ribald, drug-filled rock send-up.

When Harry Met Sally
age 14+ ★★★★☆
Wit- and charm-filled romantic-comedy classic.

Boyhood
age 15+ ★★★★★
Unique, affecting, mature drama about life and growing up.

The Breakfast Club
age 15+ ★★★★☆
Socially relevant '80s teen flick.

The Dark Knight
age 15+ ★★★★★
Excellent sequel much darker, more violent than the first.

Good Will Hunting
age 15+ ★★★★★
Moving story of brilliant, troubled youth for older teens.

The Graduate
age 15+ ★★★★★
Influential coming-of-age sex comedy.

What makes a movie a "classic"?

Moulin Rouge
age 15+ ★★★★☆
Dazzling musical romance for teens.

Psycho
age 15+ ★★★★★
Horror masterpiece definitely isn't for young kids.

Rashomon
age 15+ ★★★★★
Masterpiece about absolute truth. Best for teens.

Say Anything
age 15+ ★★★★★
A gem of a coming-of-age story.

Schindler's List ⊘ age 15+ ★★★★★
Accurate, heartbreaking masterpiece about the Holocaust.

The Shawshank Redemption ⊘ age 15+ ★★★★☆
Gritty but comforting story of friendship.

Almost Famous ⊘ age 16+ ★★★★★
Great, but lots of sex, drugs, and rock 'n' roll.

Blade Runner ⊘ age 16+ ★★★★☆
A dark, philosophical sci-fi drama for older teens.

> **Read *The Hunger Games* or the story that inspired *Blade Runner* to see how they differ from the films.**

Do the Right Thing ⊘ age 16+ ★★★★☆
Spike Lee's masterwork of racial unrest; discuss with kids.

The Godfather ⊘ age 16+ ★★★★★
The classic tale of a Mafia family, violence and all.

Network ⊘ age 16+ ★★★★★
Biting '76 satire with a media-literacy lesson.

The Pianist ⊘ age 16+ ★★★★★
True story of a Jewish pianist; OK for older kids.

Sixteen Candles ⊘ age 16+ ★★★★☆
Racy, drunken, hilarious '80s high school comedy.

Slumdog Millionaire ⊘ age 16+ ★★★★★
Epic romance-drama is brilliant but too mature for kids.

COMMON SENSE SEAL HONOREES

The Common Sense Seal is the first honor of its kind to recognize standout movies that offer an exceptional media experience for families. The Seal distinguishes titles that meet Common Sense Media's highest editorial standards for being entertaining, engaging, and effective, in addition to offering worthwhile themes, messages, and role models. The honorees of the Common Sense Seal have the potential to spark family conversations, entertain families of all types, and make a significant, lasting impact on individuals within a family or on the culture as a whole.

The Common Sense Seal honors movies rated for a wide range of ages, recognizing that families with kids at different stages are seeking appropriate, entertaining things to watch together.

The 33
Gripping, intense true ordeal of trapped Chilean miners.
age 12+ ★★★★

Above and Beyond
Stirring docu about heroic WWII pilots who aided Israel.
age 13+ ★★★★

Alexander and the Terrible, Horrible, No Good, Very Bad Day
Sweet book-based comedy has great family messages.
age 9+ ★★★★

An American Girl: Grace Stirs Up Success
Tale of young baker jam-packed with positive messages.
age 7+ ★★★★

Ant-Man
Clever, funny, cool Marvel movie has lots of sci-fi action.
age 12+ ★★★★

Antarctica: A Year on Ice
Incredible docu captures human details of remote existence.
age 9+ ★★★★

A Ballerina's Tale
Engrossing dance docu introduces powerful role model.
age 9+ ★★★★

Batkid Begins
Tremendously heartwarming, positive docu for all ages.
age 7+ ★★★★

Belle and Sebastian
Beautiful film about WWII has intense themes, drinking.
age 10+ ★★★★

Bite Size
Powerful documentary depicts obese kids' struggles.
age 10+ ★★★★

The Book of Life
Beautifully animated film has some scary imagery.
age 7+ ★★★★

The Book of Negroes
Riveting slavery epic is artful, sobering, and inspiring.
age 15+ ★★★★★

Boy and the World
Poignant hand-drawn story promotes family, environmentalism.
✓ age 7+ ★★★★

A Brave Heart: The Lizzie Velasquez Story
Outstanding role model urges kids to stand up to bullies.
✓ age 12+ ★★★★

Bridge of Spies
Cold War thriller focuses on tension over action.
✓ age 13+ ★★★★

Brooklyn
Poignant immigration drama is romantic, thought-provoking.
✓ age 14+ ★★★★★

Curious George 3: Back to the Jungle
Fast-paced, engaging sequel is fun for preschoolers.
✓ age 3+ ★★★★

Descendants
Energetic Disney movie's villains make likable role models.
✓ age 6+ ★★★★

Everest
Compelling tale of real-life expedition is intense, moving.
✓ age 12+ ★★★★

A Girl Like Her
Bullying drama is disturbing but should spark conversation.
✓ age 12+ ★★★★

The Good Dinosaur
Young dino braves nature in lovely but intense adventure.
✓ age 7+ ★★★★★

He Named Me Malala
Inspiring, deeply affecting docu explores teen icon's life.
✓ age 12+ ★★★★★

Imba Means Sing
Vibrant, uplifting docu about African children's choir.
✓ age 8+ ★★★★★

The Imitation Game
Strong performances buoy teen-friendly historical drama.
✓ age 13+ ★★★★

Inside Out
Beautiful, original story about handling big feelings.
✓ age 6+ ★★★★★

Kindness Is Contagious
Warm, feel-good docu about being nice is uplifting.

 age 9+ ★★★★

Legends of the Knight
Stirring docu sees superhero as powerful motivator for good.

age 10+ ★★★★

The Martian
Excellent space thriller mixes peril, charm, real science.

 age 12+ ★★★★

The Mask You Live In
Moving documentary examines what it means to be a man.

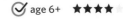 age 15+ ★★★★

McFarland, USA
Poignant story about Latino runners a winner for families.

 age 10+ ★★★★

Monkey Kingdom
Tina Fey-narrated monkey documentary is funny, educational.

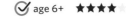 age 6+ ★★★★

Mr. Holmes
Smart, literate, low-key drama about memory and stories.

age 11+ ★★★★

Paddington
Charming story about beloved bear has some scares.

age 6+ ★★★★

Paper Planes
Thoughtful, inspired look at grief soars.

age 10+ ★★★★

Paper Towns
Smart, edgy adaptation captures the humor of self-discovery.

age 14+ ★★★★

Peanuts Emmy Honored Collection
Classic TV favorites are as charming and relevant as ever.

age 4+ ★★★★

The Peanuts Movie
Gentle family-friendly comedy has sweet messages.

age 4+ ★★★★

Red Army
Fascinating documentary about legendary Soviet hockey team.

age 9+ ★★★★

Selma ✅ age 13+ ★★★★★
Outstanding drama about MLK's fight for equal rights.

Shake the Dust ✅ age 12+ ★★★★☆
Poignant docu about B-boys and -girls around the world.

Shaun the Sheep Movie ✅ age 5+ ★★★★★
Tons of barn-animal fun in sweet stop-motion adventure.

Song of the Sea ✅ age 7+ ★★★★☆
Beautiful Irish tale explores myths, sibling relationship.

Star Wars: Episode VII: The Force Awakens ✅ age 10+ ★★★★☆
Epic Star Wars sequel delivers great performances, action.

The Tale of the Princess Kaguya ✅ age 9+ ★★★★☆
Beautifully animated Japanese folktale for older kids.

Teen Beach 2 ✅ age 8+ ★★★★☆
Dynamic musical numbers, girl power sell super sequel.

Testament of Youth ✅ age 14+ ★★★★☆
Heartrending WWI drama has heavy content, strong heroine.

This Changes Everything ✅ age 14+ ★★★★☆
Riveting climate-change docu encourages grassroots action.

Tinkerbell and the Legend of the Neverbeast ✅ age 5+ ★★★★☆
Exciting fairy adventure has loss, some scariness.

Virunga ✅ age 16+ ★★★★★
Outstanding but shattering docu set in war-torn Congo.

Walt Disney Animation Studios Short Films Collection ✅ age 5+ ★★★★★
Terrific, heartwarming shorts have something for everyone.

Zarafa ✅ age 9+ ★★★★★
Enchanting African fable with some scares and sadness.